All In Together

Classic Jump Rope Songs

Over 230 Rhymes for Fun Skipping

Edited and illustrated by Iris Moran

Published by Nona Books in 2024

First edition; First printing

Printed in the United States of America

Illustrations and design © 2024 Nona Books

www.nonabooks.com

ISBN 978 965 92935 6 8

Dedicated to all the little girls and boys who
skipped on sidewalks and chanted these
rhymes. Thanks to them, this beautiful folklore
remains alive and vibrant for the joy of
generations to come.

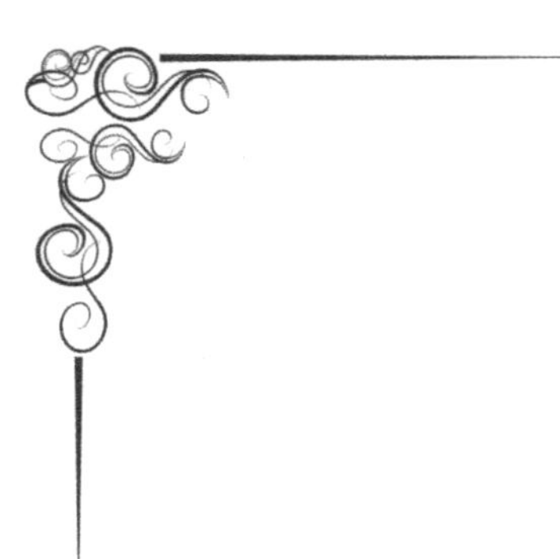

"Life is a song, sing it.
Life is a game, play it.
Life is a challenge, meet it.
Life is a dream, realize it."

-Sai Baba

Introduction

This book was created with respect and appreciation for this piece of our history, a written documentary to pass on to the next generations and strengthen the bonds within our families.

For those who grew up with skipping rhymes, we hope this book brings back sweet memories. For young readers, it offers a window to the old times, before social media was born; when chanting rhymes was a way of sharing stories.

If you happen to remember songs that are not included in this book or another variation of them, or if you want to share your experience with this book, send us an email to: info@nonabooks.com.

We would love to hear from you!

We hope this book brings joy to you and your family :-)

Happy chanting!
Nona Books team.

A Note to Parents:
The classic skipping rhymes are charming, but some of them may not reflect modern sensibilities. We've tried our best to curate and make minor adjustments to make them more kid-friendly, but there may still be some politically incorrect words. We leave it to you as a parent to decide if it's appropriate for your child or not.

TABLE OF CONTENT

TABLE OF CONTENT

Table of Content

What are Skipping Rhymes?

Before the Internet, one of the only ways people could get messages about politics, events, advertising, and gossip across to others was through chants and rhymes. They could not just create a meme and watch it go viral on social-media!

The interactive game of skipping was (and still is) enjoyed by most. Back in the day, to make it easier to get into the rhythm of the skip, those who partook in the games would chant quotes and lines from various rhymes.

Girls skipping at an athletics carnival, Australia, 1900

These chants were simply referred to as 'skipping rhymes'. They could tell a story or provide instructions for skippers; how high they should jump; how many times they should jump; what actions should be taken as they jump (like clapping hands or whistling once – toot-toot).

Some rhymes made little sense to children, but made much sense to adults. In fact, many of the rhymes with political or knowledge-sharing intent were first written by adults and then adapted to suit the kids' way of speaking at the time (kind of like emojis nowadays – kids understand them but adults, not so much)!

Some rhymes were just fun and silly for the sake of humor. Whatever the message was, skippers would recite it over and over again as they skipped, thereby delivering the message to all those who could hear them.

Jumping rope at Nambour State Rural School, Australia, 1946

Boys Started it, But Girls took it Further

Jump-rope skipping is a pastime that has been around for many centuries; likely ever since man realized how much fun it is to jump over a rope! But, in history, skipping only became recognized in Europe as a widely-accepted pastime and interactive game in the seventeenth century.

Back then girls were not allowed to show their ankles or knees, and it was considered unladylike to jump high in-front of boys. But, one century later, girls found a way around this (they wanted to have fun, too, of course), and they added their creative touch by incorporating the rhymes and chants.

Soon the girls took charge; they owned the rope (which was often one of their mothers' washing-lines), controlled the game, and decided who would and would not participate.

Pierre-Auguste Renoir, 1876
Girl with a Jump Rope
(Portrait of Delphine Legrand)
oil on canvas

The rhymes they sang would help them to keep count of each jump, sometimes even making them jump faster or higher as they recited a funny or important poem loudly and in unison.

Toward the end of the nineteenth century in the United States, when people moved to the cities in their masses, it was the girls who dominated the jump-rope skipping pastime. In the cities, the new sidewalks and roads were paved smoothly; just perfect for skipping!

Children jumping rope on the White House lawn, 1964

There Were Different Types of Rhymes, Too!

Much like nursery rhymes, jump-rope rhymes use end-words that sound the same phonically, with a select number of syllables to help keep the 'beat' of the game.

Some jump-rope skipping rhymes feature the use of counting numbers, allowing the jumper to keep time and to keep tabs on how many successful jumps the skipper has made.

Some rhymes, known as 'Hot Pepper' rhymes, keep the skipper jumping really fast!

Most of the classic rhymes were created by young girls from the United Kingdom, United States of America, and Ireland. As these girls traveled from country to country through social expansion, so they took their rhymes with them and introduced them to new audiences, from sidewalk to sidewalk and schoolyard to schoolyard.

Much like memes and social media posts are shared among teenagers today, these classic rhymes were mostly created by and shared between children, as opposed to being shared from adults to children.

Good for Coordination!

Like tennis or soccer, jump-rope skipping while singing a rhyming song certainly helps to develop hand, eye, and foot coordination.
Keeping body and muscular movements in time with the spoken words strengthens communication between the nervous-system and the mind, which improves overall cognitive function – placing the skipper in charge of their own movements and choices.

This in turn develops one's creative-thinking abilities. When beneficial motor patterns become second nature, we have more time and a stronger mental ability to think outside of the box. Also, some of the nonsensical rhymes that are recited help to open the mind to new ways of thinking, too!

There are, of course, physical strength benefits as well; increasing stamina while building foot and leg muscles.

Jump-rope skipping while singing skipping rhymes has also been proven to improve memory and keen learning in young children. So, it's true that singing is good for the soul!

Finally!

we have gathered a number of jump-rope skipping rhymes and activities from around the world. The purpose of this book is to share these with you, and we're pretty sure they're going to bring you hours of fun and laughter, and a healthy body, too!

So, go ahead and fill your day with silly-singing and jolly-jumping! And, hey – after that - you may even want to create your own skipping rhythm and rhyme!

Have fun!

Illustrated by Friedrich August Mottu, July 1815,
Collection Metropolitan Museum of Art

HOT PEPPERS

"Red Hot Peppers" in jump rope songs means the rope swings super fast, like how spicy peppers feel super hot. It's a way to make the game trickier because you have to jump really fast to not get caught by the rope. Think of it as turning the speed way up and seeing if you can keep up without tripping. This fast jumping game is a cool challenge to test how quick and nimble you can be, making it extra fun and exciting compared to slower jump rope games. It's a favorite way to play with friends at school or the park, helping you get better at jumping and staying on your toes!

"Red Hot Peppers" is typically for advanced jumpers. It requires quick feet, good timing, and lots of practice to keep up with the fast-turning rope without missing a jump. It's a fun challenge for those who have mastered the basics of jump rope and are ready to take on something trickier!

My Grandfather's Farm

As I went down to
my grandfather's farm.
A Billy goat chased me
around the barn.

It chased me up
a sycamore tree,
And this is what
it said to me:

"Down by the water where the green grass grows
There sat (name of jumper) as sweet as a rose.
He/She sang, he/she sang, he/she sang so sweet;
Along came his/her girl-friend/boy-friend
And kissed him/her on the cheek.
How many kisses did he/she get?
One, two, three, four, etc."

Rope is turned faster and faster until there is a miss.

Paul, Do You Love Me?

Paul, Paul, do you love me?
(replace Paul with any other name)
"Yes, no, maybe so!"

Then the rope is turned very fast till a jumper misses.

Help (1)

Players call out the letters of HELP as they jump over and over. The ropes spin faster and faster until a jumper misses a letter. Then, the jumper who missed must perform the action associated with that missed letter. Another option is for the next jumper to perform the action of the missed letter.

H - E - L - P
One jump for each letter

H - Highwaters
The rope doesn't touch the ground

E - Eyes closed or Easy over
The rope goes over slower than usual

L - Leapfrog
Jump like a frog, then jump high

P - Peppers
The rope twirls quickly

Help (2)

H - hot pepper
The rope goes fast

E - elevator
The rope goes up

L - limbo
The rope goes down when she comes out

P - popcorn
You wiggle the rope & the jumper has to go under it

My Father was a Butcher

My father was a butcher,
My mother cut the meat,
And I'm a little wienie
That runs around the street.
How many times did I run around the street?
One, two, three, four, etc.

Rope is turned faster and faster till skipper missed.

Motor Boat

Motor boat motor boat:
go so slow.
Turn jump rope slow

Motor boat, motor boat:
go a little faster.
Turn jump rope normal speed

Motor boat, motor boat:
step on the gas!
Turn jump rope at high speed

Up & Down the Ladder

Old man lazy
Drives me crazy.
Up the ladder.
Jumper moves toward an end

Down the ladder.
Jumper moves toward the other end

'Till it gets H-O-T (spell hot).
Turn jump rope at high speed

On the Beach

On the beach,
in the sand,
I jump up & down,
oh so grand!
On the beach,
I turn around,
On the beach,
a shell I found
On the beach,
I get tan,
On the beach
in the sand,
it's Hot, hot, hot!

turn rope faster and faster!

Red Hot Peppers

Red hot peppers
speed up the jump rope.
Let's see how fast we can go
10, 20, 30, 40, 50, 60, 70,
80, 90, 100 and out I go!

*As the kids sing the song, the ones on the end
turning the rope start moving it faster and faster.
The jumper tries to keep up with the speed and
counts by tens. If they get to 100, they jump out and
someone else jumps in.*

Mississippi

How do you spell Mississippi?
"M"
cross arms over chest
"I"
point to your eye
"S" Crooked letter
cross legs and jump
"S" Crooked letter
cross legs and jump
"I"
point to eye
"S" Crooked letter
cross legs and jump
"S" Crooked letter
cross legs and jump
"I"
point to eye
"P" Hunch back
"P" Hunch back
"I"!

Mrs. Sippi lives by the shore,
She has children three and four,
The oldest one is twenty-four.
She shall marry:
rope is turned very fast
Rich man, poor man,
Beggar-man, thief,
Doctor, lawyer,
Merchant, chief,
Tinker, tailor,
Cowboy.

Red Hot

Red Hot Pepper,
In the pot,
Gotta get over
what the leaders got.
10, 20, 30, 40, ...

The turners turn the rope faster until the jumper misses.
Keep an eye on the scores and see who has the highest score.

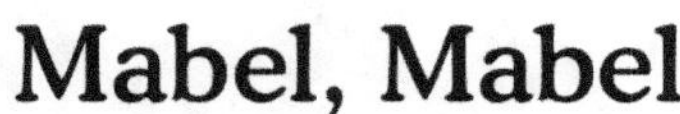

Mabel, Mabel

This is a true classic. This rhyme is intended to test the coordination of the jumper by turning the rope faster and faster.

Mabel, Mabel, set the table,
Just as fast as you are able.
Don't forget the salt, sugar, vinegar, mustard,
red-hot pepper!

Mabel, Mabel, neat and able.
Mabel, Mabel, set the table,
And don't forget the
Red Hot Peppers!

Mabel, Mabel, set the table.
Don't forget the red hot label.
Shake the salt and shake the pepper.
Who will be the highest stepper?
Winds blow hot and winds blow freeze,
How many times did Mabel sneeze?
One, two, three . . . . .
Repeat the words salt, pepper, vinegar, mustard as the rope is being turned. If the jumper misses their jump on the word 'pepper' the rope spinners start turning the rope faster or begin doing 'hot peppers'.

Mrs. Pink

Mrs Pink fell in the sink
How many litres did she drink?
1,2,3,4,
Turn rope faster and faster.

Down by the River

Down by the river,
down by the sea,
Johnny broke a bottle
and blamed it on me.
I told ma, ma told pa,

Johnny got a spanking
so ha ha ha.
How many spankings
did Johnny get?
1, 2, 3....

Turn the rope faster and faster, and continue counting until the jumper misses and that will be the answer.

High, Low, Medium, Slow

High, low, medium, slow,
Jolly ol' pepper and away we go!
Turn the rope according to the words:
"High"
The skipping rope is a foot off the ground,
"Low"
The skipper bends down to skip,
"Medium"
Normal skipping,
"Slow"
Slow skipping,
"Pepper"
Very fast skipping.

BIRTHDAY RHYMES

In birthday jump rope games, the singing includes everyone calling out the months from January to December. If you're playing, you need to listen carefully. When the month you were born in is called out, that's your signal to jump into the moving rope and start skipping. You have to be quick and jump in at just the right moment so you can keep up with the rope without stopping it. The game lasts until December is called, or until someone's foot gets caught on the rope. It's a cool way to make the skipping special for each one of the players.

All in Together Girls (1)

All in together girls
It's fine weather girls
When is your birthday
Please jump in

The next part is said very fast:

January, February, March, April,
May, June, July, August,
September, October,
November, December

All out together girls
It's fine weather girls
When is your birthday?
Please jump out
1, 2, 3, 4, 5, 6, 7, 8, 9, 10, 11, 12, 13, 14, 15,...

Each jumper runs in when they hear the month of their birthday. Then the months repeated, and each person jumps out on their birthday month.

All in Together Girls (2)

All in together girls,
Never mind the weather girls,
When I call your birthday,
You must jump in,

January, February,
March, April, May, June,
July, August, September,
October, November, December!
The skipper jumps in when their birthday month is called.

Apples, Peaches, Pears and Plums

Apples, peaches, pears, and plums
Tell me when your birthday comes:
January, February, March, April,
May, June, July, August, September,
October, November, December?
*The skipper jumps in when their birthday month is
called.*

Then start counting:
1, 2, 3, 4, 5, 6, 7, 8, 9, 10, 11, 12, etc.
*The skipper jumps out when they reach the day of
their birthday.*

All in together kids

All in together kids
Never mind the weather kids
When it's your birthday please jump out!
January, February, March, April, May June… etc
children jump out as the month of birthday is called.

Sheep in the meadow

Sheep in the meadow,
Cows in the corn.
Jump in on the month that you were born.
January, February, March, April…
*Jumpers jump out as the month of their birthday is
called, Or start jumping in & jumping out on the month
of their birthday.*

Can You Find the Hidden Phrase?

☐	Five Little Monkeys, 9, 4
☐	The Wind, The Wind, 5, 2
☐	Rich man Poor Man (1), 17, 8
☐	Banana, Banana, Banana Split, 3, 4
☐	Jelly in the Dish, 6, 3
☐	I Love, 4, 4
☐	Lemon Lime, 5, 1
☐	All in Together Girls, 3, 2
☐	Rich man Poor Man (1), 17, 8
☐	Rooms for Rent, 2, 2
☐	Birdie, Birdie in the Sky , 3, 4
☐	Eleanor, 8, 3

For example: play   Anna Banana, 3, 4

Anna Banana
1. Anna Banana
2. Plays the piano.
3. All she can play
4. Is, "The Star Spangled Banner".
5. Anna, Banana Split!

3rd line,
4th word

COUNTING RHYMES

Counting rhymes are great for keeping track of how many jumps you make without tripping. Typically (but not always), these rhymes start with a question followed by counting. The counting stops when you reach a certain number or when someone misses the rope. Whatever number you stop at is the answer to the question. Sometimes the questions are silly or embarrassing in a harmless way, which makes the game even more fun! So, get ready to hop, skip, and count along with these rhymes! They'll make skipping even more exciting and challenging!

I Made a Wish Jumping Rope

I made a wish jumping rope,
I caught a fish jumping rope,
I gave a kiss jumping rope,
How many wishes did I get?
1, 2, 3, ...
How many fish did I get?
1, 2, 3, ...
How many kisses did I get?
1, 2, 3, ...

Just Have Some Fun

One - just have some fun.
Two- tie your shoe.
Three - I am free.
Four - walk out the door.
Five - kick a beehive.
Six - throw some sticks.
Seven - cya in heaven.
Eight - you are late.
Nine - let the sunshine.
Ten -
Say a jumper's name, now jump out.

Bread and Butter

Bread and butter
Sugar and spice
How many boys Think I am nice?
None, one, two, three….

7-Up

Show off your counting skills and flexibility with this one. Perform the actions of each line.

7 up, 7 up, count to 11 up
1 2 3, 4 5 6, 7 8 9 10 11
6 up, 6 up, do the splits up
1, 2, 3, 4, 5, 6
5 up, 5 up, touch the side up
1, 2, 3, 4, 5
4 up, 4 up, touch the floor up
1, 2, 3, 4
3 up, 3 up, touch your knee up
1, 2, 3
2 up, 2 up, touch your shoe up
1, 2
1 up, 1 up, you're all done up

Sixteen Bluebirds

Sixteen bluebirds sitting on a fence.
Flapped their wings and started to dance.
Upward, downward,
All along the line,
Brightly preened and looking fine!
Count 1, 2, 3 . . . . .

Hickety Pickety Pop

Hickety Pickety Pop,
How many times before I stop?
1, 2, 3, 4, 5, 6, 7, 8, 9, 10, . . .

Cinderella

This is one of the most popular skipping rhymes. Begin by swinging the rope back and forth rather than overhead. Once the counting part begins, switch to swinging the rope overhead.

To provide a bigger challenge, count by twos, threes or multiples of a given number.

Cinderella, dressed in green,
Went upstairs to eat ice cream.
How many spoonfuls did she eat?
One, two, three, four, five, six,
seven, eight.

Cinderella, dressed in black,
Went upstairs and sat on a tack.
How many stitches did it take?
One, two, three, four, five, six,
seven, eight.

Cinderella, dressed in yellow,
Went upstairs to kiss her fellow.
Made a mistake
And kissed a snake
Came downstairs
With a bellyache.
How many doctors did it take?
One, two, three, four, five, six,
seven, eight.

Cinderella, dressed in yellow,
Went downtown to buy some mustard.
On the way, her girdle busted.
How many people were disgusted?
One, two, three, four, five, six,
seven, eight.

Cinderella, dressed in yellow
Went to town to mail a letter
On the way she met her fellow.
How many kisses did she get?
One, two, three, four, five, six,
seven, eight.

Cinderella, dressed in pink
Washed the dished in the sink.
How many dishes did she break?
One, two, three, four, five, six,
seven, eight.

Cinderella, dressed in green
Died last night at seven fifteen.
How many cars came to her funeral?
One, two, three, four, five, six,
seven, eight.

Cinderella, dressed in brown
Went upstairs to make a gown
How many stitches did she use?
One, two, three, four, five, six,
seven, eight.

Cinderella, dressed in rose
Went upstairs to powder her nose.
How many boxes did she use?
One, two, three, four, five, six,
seven, eight.

Mickey Mouse

Mickey Mouse,
Built a house,
How many bricks,
Did he use?

One, two, three,
four, five, six...

Fishing

Fishing Down by the river,
Down by the sea.
Let's go fishing just you & me!
How many fish will there be?
One, two, three, four, five….?

Had a Little Bumper Car

Had a little bumper car, number 48,
went around the cor --
skipper jumps out and runs around the twirler and run back in the rope. Keep saying 'corner' until the skipper jumps back in.
--ner
and slams on the brakes.
Policeman came and put me in jail.
How many days did he put me in jail?
1, 2, 3, 4, 5, 6….
Count until the jumper misses and that will be the answer.

Down In the Meadow Down

 in the meadow,
Where the green grass grows,
There sat (*say jumper's name*)
As sweet as a rose.
She sang and she sang
And she sang so sweet,
Along came a butterfly
And kissed her on the cheek.
Another flew across
And kissed her on the nose.
How many times can she jump on her toes?
One, two, three, etc.

Salad

With Salad I am sick,
With salad I am sick,
With celery I am cured,
How many stalks of celery,
One, two, three . . . . .

Cross the River

Cross the river
Cross the lake
I hope I don't make
a bad mistake!
How many jumps will I take?

Big Ben

This chant was documented in London during the 1950s.

Big Ben strikes one,
Big Ben strikes two,
Big Ben strikes three,
Big Ben strikes four,
Big Ben strikes five,
etc.

Blondie

Blondie and Dagwood
Went to town.
Blondie bought
An evening gown.
Dagwood bought
A pair of shoes.
Cookie stayed home
To watch the news.
And this is what is said:
Close your eyes
Jumper closes eyes
Count to ten, if you miss a number
take an end!
One, two, three, four, five, six,
seven, eight, nine, ten!

Hello, Hello, Hello Sir

Each time the players say "Sir," the jumper touches the ground with his or her.

Hello, hello, hello, sir.
Meet me at the grocer,
No, sir. Why, sir?
Because I have a cold, sir,
Where did you get the cold, sir?
At the North Pole, sir,
What were you doing there, sir?
Counting polar bears, sir,
How many did you count, sir?
One, two, three, four, five . . . .

Cookies, Candies in a Dish

Cookies, candy in the dish,
How many pieces do you wish?
1, 2, 3, 4, . . .

Chickety, Chickety, Chop

Chickety, Chickety,
Chop Chickety,
chickety, chop.
How many times before I stop?
One, two three, four, five…..?

My Little Sister

My Little Sister
My little sister
dressed in pink
Washed all the dishes
in the sink.
How many went "clink, clink, clink"?
One, two three, four five…?

Robin Hood

Robin Hood, Robin Hood dressed so good,
Robin Hood, Robin Hood dressed so good,
Got as many kisses as he could.
How many kisses did he get?
1, 2, 3 . . . . .

Spider and Cider

Applesauce, mustard, cider,
How many legs has a spider?
one, two, three, etc.

Chocolate Cake

My mother made
a chocolate cake.
How many eggs
did it take?
One, two, three, four, five…

I Eat My Peas with Honey

I eat my peas with honey,
I've done it all my life,
It looks a little funny,
But it keeps them on my knife,
How many peas can I get on my knife?
1, 2, 3, . . .

Cinderella dressed in Yella

Cinderella dressed in Yella
Went downtown to meet her fella
On the way her girdle busted
How many people were disgusted
5-10-15-20-25-30…

Eggy Peggy

Eggy Peggy
Lost her leggy
Sliding down a chucky eggy
How many eggs did she smash?
1,2,3,4……..

First Grade Babies (1)

This version is from people who grew up in the west side of Chicago in the 1930's-40's.

First grade babies,
Second grade tots,
Third grade angels,
Fourth grade snots,
Fifth grade peaches,
Sixth grade plums,
Seventh grade ladies,
Eighth grade bums!

First grade babies,
Second grade tots,
Third grade angels,
Fourth grade snots,
Fifth grade peaches,
Sixth grade plums,
Seventh grade dummy,
Eighth grade bums.

First Grade Peaches/Babies (2)

This version is coming from Minnesota:

First grade babies,
Second grade brats,
Third grade angels,
Fourth grade rats,
Fifth grade peaches,
Sixth grade plums,
And all the rest
are dirty bums!

First grade babies,
Second grade tots,
Third grade angels,
Fourth grade snots,
Fifth grade peaches,
Sixth grade pears,
and all the rest
are great big bears.

First-grade peaches,
Second-grade plums,
Tell me when
your birthday comes!
January, February, March, April, May,
June, etc.
Then you stop when the month of the jumper
comes, and then you start on dates:

1, 2, 3, 4, 5, 6, 7, 8, etc.
and when the person's date comes up, the
jumper jumps out.

First grade babies,
Second grade tots,
Third grade angels,
Fourth grade snots,
Fifith grade peaches,
Sixth grade plums,
Seventh grade hard workers,
Eighth grade bums.

Bluebells, Cockle Shells

Bluebells, cockle shells,
Eevie, ivy, over;
I like coffee, I like tea;
I like the boys, and the boys like me.

Tell your mother to hold her tongue;
She met a fellow when she was young.
Tell your father to do the same;
He met a girl and he changed her name.

Bluebells, cockle shells,
Eevie, ivy, over;
Mother went to market
To buy some meat;

Baby's in the cradle
Fast asleep.
The old clock on the mantel says:
One o'clock, two o'clock,
three o'clock, four o'clock,
five o'clock, six o'clock,
seven o'clock, eight o'clock,
nine o'clock, ten o'clock,
eleven o'clock, twelve o'clock.

ALPHABET RHYMES

Alphabet skipping rhymes offer a lively twist to traditional skipping by incorporating the ABCs into the fun! With each letter of the alphabet corresponding to a jump, you'll not only sharpen your letter recognition but also enhance your coordination and rhythm. As you skip along, the counting stops either when someone misses the rope or when you reach the last letter of the alphabet. Some songs even include questions about someone, and the letter where the counting stops reveals the answer – the first letter of that person's name. This can lead to amusing and sometimes embarrassing moments in a lighthearted way! So, gather your friends and get ready to hop, skip, and giggle your way through the alphabet!

A My Name is Alice

A A my name is ALICE, my husband's name is AL,
we live in ALABAMA and we sell ARTICHOKES.

B B my name is BETTY, my husband's name is BEN,
we live in BERMUDA and we sell BICYCLES.

C C my name is CAROL, my husband's name is CARL,
we live in COLORADO and we sell CUCUMBERS.

D D my name is DIANE, my husband's name is DAVID,
we live in DENVER and we sell DOUGHNUTS.

E E my name is ELIZABETH, my husband's name is ETHAN,
we live in ENGLAND and we sell EARRINGS.

F F my name is FIONA, my husband's name is FRANK,
we live in FLORIDA and we sell FLIP-FLOPS.

G G my name is GERTRUDE, my husband's name is GARY,
we live in GEORGIA and we sell GRAPES.

H H my name is HARRIET, my husband's name is HENRY,
we live in HAWAII and we sell HATS.

I I my name is ISOBEL, my husband's name is ISSAC,
we live in IDAHO and we sell ICE-CREAM.

J J my name is JULIE, my husband's name is JACK,
we live in JAPAN and we sell JAM.

K my is KATE, my husband's name is KEVIN,
we live in KENTUCKY and we sell KITES.

L my name is LINDA, my husband is LEONARD,
we live in LOUISIANA and we sell LADDERS.

M my name is MARY, my husband's name is MARK,
we live in MICHIGAN and we sell MATS.

N my name is NICOLA, my husband's name is NIGEL,
we live in NEBRASKA and we sell NECKLACES.

O my name is OLIVIA, my husband's name is OSCAR,
we live in OHIO and we sell ONIONS.

P my name is PENNY, my husband's name is PETER,
we live in PENNSYLVANIA and we sell PEANUTS.

Q my name is QUEENIE, my husband's name is QUENTIN,
we live in QUEBEC and we sell QUILTS.

R my name is RUBY, my husband's name is ROBERT,
we live in ROMANIA and we sell RHUBARB.

S my name is SARAH, my husband's name is SIMON,
we live in SOUTH CAROLINA and we sell SPOONS.

T my name is TABITHA, my husband's name is TONY,
we live in TEXAS and we sell TOYS.

U my name is URSULA, my husband's name is ULRICH,
we live in UTAH and we sell UMBRELLAS.

V my name is VIOLET, my husband's name is VICTOR,
we live in VERMONT and we sell VASES.

W my name is WANDA, my husband's name is WILLIAM,
we live in WASHINGTON and we sell WATCHES.

X my name is XENA, my husband's name is XAVIER,
we live in XIANYANG and we sell XYLOPHONES.

Y my name is YASMIN, my husband's name is YORICK,
we live in YEMEN and we sell YACHTS.

Z my name is ZOE, my husband's name is ZANDLER,
we live in ZAMBIA and we sell ZIPS.

Down the Mississippi

To make a bigger challenge spell out M-i-s-s-i-s-s-i-p-p-i while jumping.

Spell Mississippi
With a capital M - I
Crooked letter, crooked letter - i -
Crooked letter, crooked letter - i -
Hump backed, hump backed - i -
Down the Mississippi
Where the steamboats push.

*The second jumper next in line runs in
and gently pushes the jumper out.*

Apple Tart

Raspberry, strawberry, apple jam tart.
Tell me the name of your sweetheart.
A, B, C, D, ….

The rope must turn very fast as the alphabet is being said, the person jumping shouts the name of a boy or of a girl that he/she likes. Their name must start with the letter that was being said at the time.

A, B, C and Vegetable Soup

A, B, C and Vegetable Soup,
What will I find in my alphabet soup?
A, B, C. . . . .

When a letter is missed. Think of a word beginning with the same letter that was missed.

Peel a Banana

The two holding the rope sing:
Peel a banana upside down
see if you can touch the ground
if you spell your name correct,
you will get another chance.

The jumper then spells their name, one letter for each jump, and tries to touch the ground with each letter without being tripped by the rope.
If the jumper trips or messes up the spelling, it's another jumper's turn.

Ice Cream Soda (1)

Ice cream soda, cherry on the top,
Who's your boyfriend/girlfriend I forgot
A, B, C, D, E, F, G, H, ...
Carry on the alphabet until the jumper stops. Take the letter they stop on and name a friend with that letter at the beginning of their name.

Ice Cream Soda (2)

Ice cream soda,
Lemonade punch.
Tell me the name
Of my honey-bunch
A, B, C, D, E...

When the jumper misses, the players call a name beginning with the letter in which the jumper missed. This name will indicate the first letter of the name of the jumper's sweetheart. Then the skipping is resumed.

Out Goes the Rat

Out goes the rat
Out goes the cat
Out goes the lady
With the big green hat
Y, O, U, spells you
O, U, T spells out!

GLOOMY RHYMES

Most skipping songs are all about fun and laughter, but there are a few that talk about sadder things too. These songs remind us that life isn't always happy-go-lucky and that it's okay to feel sad sometimes. They might talk about losing a pet or feeling lonely, but they help us understand that everyone goes through tough times. So, when you're skipping along and singing these songs, remember that it's okay to feel sad, and that singing and jumping can help us feel better when we're feeling down.

Last Night and the Night Before

Last night,
night before,
my boyfriend took me
to the candy store.
on the word "store" the jumper turns around to face the opposite direction that they started out in.

He bought me ice cream,
he bought me a cake.
He brought me home
with a belly ache.

Mamma, mamma, I feel sick.
Call the doctor quick, quick quick!
jump on one foot each time you say "quick".

Doctor, Doctor will I die?
Close your eyes and count to 5.
1...2...3...4...5..

on 5 the jumper jumps out of the rope while the rope turners are still singing.
I'm still alive and on channel 5!

Here I am Little Jumping Joan

Here am I, little jumping Joan,
When nobody's with me,
I'm always alone.

I Had a Little Brother

This song also has an alternative version that refers to a sister instead of a brother.

I had a little brother,
And his name was Johnny,
He played in the meadow,
Where the frogs croaked funny,
He ran through the meadow,
With a song on his tongue,
And he picked a few flowers
Just for fun.
How many flowers did he find?
1, 2, 3 . . . .

Banana, Banana

This song is from the Boston area.

Banana, banana
Banana split!
Mama bought
a newborn chick!
Chickie died.
Mama cried.
Banana, banana
Banana split!

My Mother Said I Never Should

The song is sung to the tune of "Go In and Out the Window".

My mother said,
I never should
Play with the
gypsies in the wood.
If I did, she would say:
'Naughty girl to disobey!'

My mother said
I never should
Play with the
gypsies in the wood.
The wood was dark,
the grass was green;
By came Sally with a tambourine.

Don't Worry

Don't worry
If your job is small
And your rewards are few.
Just remember
The mighty oak
Was once a nut like you.

Found a Peanut

Found a peanut,
Found a peanut,
Found a peanut last night,
Last night I found a peanut,
Found a peanut last night.

It was rotten,
It was rotten,
It was rotten last night,
Last night it was rotten,
It was rotten last night.

Ate it anyway,
Ate it anyway,
Ate it anyway last night,
Last night I ate it anyway,
Ate it anyway last night.

Got a tummy ache,
Got a tummy ache,
Got a tummy ache last night,
Last night I got a tummy ache,
Got a tummy ache last night.

Went to the hospital,
Went to the hospital,
Went to the hospital last night,
Last night I went to the hospital,
Went to the hospital last night.

Took some medicine,
Took some medicine,
Took some medicine last night,
Last night I took some medicine,
Took some medicine last night.

Felt better,
Felt better,
Felt better last night,
Last night I felt better,
I felt better last night.

TIP 

When *is* the Right Time
to Enter the Rope

The right time to enter the rope is when it's just about to pass over your head. A helpful tip to recognize the right time is to listen for the sound of the rope as it hits the ground. As soon as you hear the "whoosh" sound, it means the rope is about to come up again, so that's your cue to jump in!

JUMP IN, JUMP OUT

Jump In, Jump Out rhymes are super fun skipping songs that get you moving and jumping around with your friends. In these rhymes, you have to listen carefully to the chant and jump in or out of the rope at just the right time. It's like a cool dance routine but with a skipping rope! It's even more fun when you play with a group because you all have to jump together and stay in sync. Jumping in means you have to hop into the rope while it's swinging around without tripping, which can be a bit tricky but super exciting once you get the hang of it. And when it's time to jump out, you've got to exit the rope smoothly without getting tangled up. It's all about timing and teamwork while encouraging friendship and healthy competition!

Benjamin Franklin Went to France

This rhyme shows the awareness of children back then to World War II. The Queen in the song is probably Queen Elizabeth who ruled during this period.

Benjamin Franklin went to France,
To teach the ladies how to dance,
First on the heels,
touch your heel
Then on the toes,
touch your toe
Around and around and around you go,
turn around
Salute to the Captain,
mimic a salute
Bow to the Queen,
mimic a bow
Touch the bottom of the submarine.
And turn your back on the Nazi submarine!

Calling In, Calling Out

The jumper shouts out the name of another jumper and exits. The other jumper jumps in and continues the same with a third jumper, and so on.

Calling in, calling out,
(*say another jumper's name*) runs in
when I run out!
The first jumper exists, and the second jumper jumps in.

Rooms for Rent

Rooms for rent,
Rooms for rent,
Enquire within,
As I move out,
Let (*say jumper's name*) come in.
The next jumper jumps in.

Granny was in
the Kitchen

Granny was in the kitchen
doing a bit of stitching
One player is jumping
When in came a bogie man
and pushed her out
*A second player joins in skipping and
replaces the first by pushing them out*

Apartment for Rent

Apartment for rent,
inquire within,
When (*jumpers' name*) moves out,
Jumper jumps out
let (*another jumpers' name*) in
the other jumper jumps in

There's Someone Under the Bed

There's someone under the bed
Whoever can it be?
I feel really frightened
So (*jumper's name*) comes in with me
jumper jumps in
First we light the candle
Then we look and see
Oh (*jumper's name*) go out,
(*jumper's name*) go out
jumper jumps out
And leave the rest to me.
Rhyme continues, jumpers take turns.

My Mother Caught a Flea

1, 2, 3, my mother caught a flea,
She put it in the teapot
and made a cup of tea,
The flea jumped out,
My mother gave a shout,
And in came a bobby
with his shirt hanging out.

Mother, Mother

Mother, Mother, I am ill
Call for the doctor over the hill.
In came the doctor,
First jumper jumps in

In came the nurse,
Second jumper jumps in

In came the lady with the alligator purse.
Third jumper jumps in

"Measles," said the doctor.
"Mumps," said the nurse.
"Nothing," said the lady with the alligator purse.
Out goes the doctor,
First jumper jumps out

out goes the nurse,
Second jumper jumps out

Out goes the lady with the alligator purse.
Third jumper jumps out

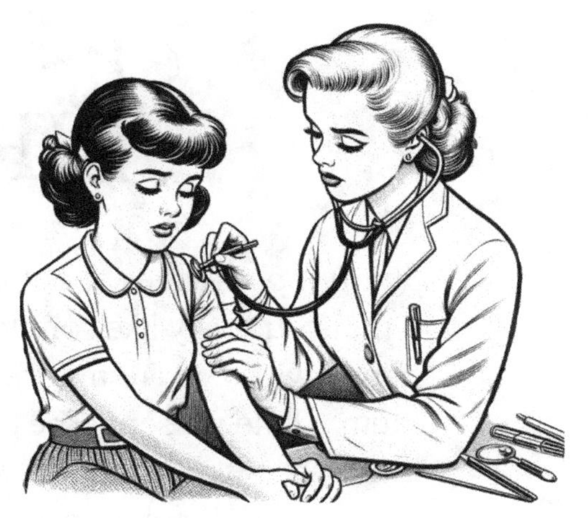

House to let

House to let,
apply within
When Josh goes out
Ava comes in
name a jumper, and continue taking turns.

FIRST LOVE

Jump rope rhymes about first love are all about those butterflies you get when you really like someone. They talk about holding hands, feeling happy when you're around that special person, and maybe even giving them a little present. These rhymes make you feel all warm and fuzzy inside, like when you see your crush smiling at you across the playground. Singing these songs was a way for kids to share their feelings without feeling too shy or embarrassed about it.

Apples and Pears

This one is super fun (especially the kicking part).

Johnny gave me apples,
Johnny gave me pears,
Johnny gave me fifty cents,
To kiss him on the stairs.

I gave him back his apples,
I gave him back his pears,
I gave him back his fifty cents,
And kicked him down the stairs.

Down in the Valley

Begin by swinging the rope back and forth rather than overhead. Once the counting part
begins, switch to swinging the rope overhead.

Down in the valley,
Where the green grass grows,
Sat little Annie,
As sweet as a rose,
Along came a boy,
And whispered on her ear,
Why, Annie, you ought to be ashamed!
Got a little boyfriend,
And you don't know his name!
What is his name?
A, B, C ...

K-I-S-S-I-N-G

This is one of the most popular classic rhymes. Replace the jumper and their sweetheart names with Janey or Johnny.

Janey and Johnny,
Sitting in a tree,
K-I-S-S-I-N-G,
First comes love,
Then comes marriage
Then comes Janey,
With a baby carriage.

Love is Bliss

Ann is angry.
Bob is bad.
Helen is hateful.
Sam is sad.
I'm in love
And love is bliss.
How many times do I kiss?
One, two, three, ...
Continue counting

I Love the Boys

I love coffee,
I love tea,
I love the boys,
And the boys love me.

Pretty Little Dutch Girl

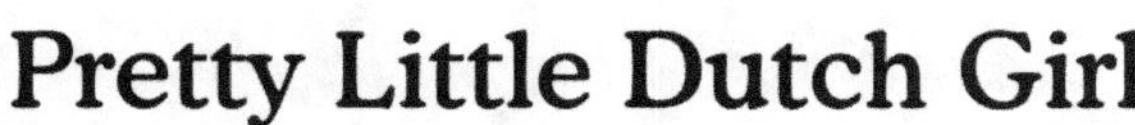

This song has many different versions. The earliest recorded version comes from New York around 1940, and there have been versions up to 2010. The version below is from the USA, Columbus, Ohio in the 1970s. It became popular across the United States by the 1950s and reached Britain in 1959, where it quickly became one of the most popular skipping rhymes among girls.

The rhyme tells the story of a very beautiful Dutch girl who is popular with boys. She has a boyfriend who isn't as attractive. Some versions say that the boyfriend leaves the pretty Dutch girl for an even prettier girl.

I am a pretty little Dutch girl,
As pretty as can be.
And all the boys in my home town,
Go crazy over me.
I have a boyfriend name Tony,
who comes from Land of Baloney.
With 48 toes and a pickle on his nose,
And that's the way my story goes.
One day as I was walking,
I heard my boyfriend talking.
To a pretty little girl with strawberry curls,
And this is what he said to her.
I L-O-V-E, love you,
I K-I-S-S, kiss you.
In a D-A-R-K, D-A-R-K, dark, dark room.

I Love

One I love, Two I Love,
One I love, Two I love,
Three I love I say,
With all my heart,
Five I cast away.
Six he loves, Seven she loves,
Eight they both love,
Nine he comes, Ten he carries,
Eleven he courts, Twelve he marries.

The Wind, The Wind

The Wind, The Wind,
The Wind, The Wind,
The Wind blows high,
It blows Mary through the sky,
She is fair and she is pretty,
She is the girl from the tin can city,
She can play the piano, 1 2 3,

Mary, Mary, who is she?
Johnny, Johnny says he loves her,
Off they go with a kiss, kiss, kiss,
He took her to the courtyard,
Asked her,
Will you marry me?
Yes, No, Maybe so,
Yes, No, Maybe so.

I'll Tell Me Ma

This song also called "The Wind" or "The Belle of Belfast City". It was collected in various parts of England in the 19th century.

I'll tell me ma,
when I get home
The boys won't
leave the girls alone
Pulled my hair,
and stole my comb
But that's all right, till I go home.

She is handsome,
she is pretty
She is the belle of
(*say your city name*) city
She is a-courting one, two, three
Pray, can you tell me who is she?

Strawberry Shortcake (1)

Strawberry shortcake,
Huckleberry pie,
who's gonna be your lucky guy,
a, b, c, d, e, f, g etc.

*continue until the jumper misses and think of a
name that begins with that letter. The chosen name
would be the lucky guy.*

Strawberry Shortcake (2)

Strawberry Shortcake
Strawberry shortcake,
cream on top,
Tell me the name of your sweetheart?
Is it Alex, Brandon, Cam, Danielle, ...?

My Boyfriend's Name is Fatty

My boyfriend's name is Fatty,
He comes from Cincinatti,
With 48 toes
And a dimple on his nose,
And this is how my story goes:
I L-O-V-E love him,
I'll K-I-S-S kiss him,
I'll H-U-G hug him
In the p-a-r-k park park park.
My boyfriend gave me peaches.
My boyfriend gave me pears.
My boyfriend gave me 50 cents
to kiss him on the stairs.
I gave him back his peaches.
I gave him back his pears.
I gave him back his 50 cents
And kicked him down the stairs.

TIP

How to Turn the Rope
the Right Way

1. **Keep it Steady:** Swing the rope at a steady pace, not too fast and not too slow.
2. **Use Your Wrists:** Focus on using your wrists to turn the rope, rather than your whole arm. It's like making small circles with your wrists.
3. **Coordinate with the jumper:** Sync your turns with the jumper's rhythm to maintain a steady pace and prevent the rope from hitting the jumper's feet or body.
4. **Stay focused:** Avoid distractions to ensure consistent and efficient turning.
5. **Maintain the proper distance:** Stand at an appropriate distance from the jumper to ensure the rope's arc is consistent and doesn't interfere with the jumper's movements.
6. **Remember**: mastering rope turning takes practice. Don't get discouraged if you can't do it perfectly right away. Keep practicing, and soon enough, you'll improve your skills and become a pro rope turner!

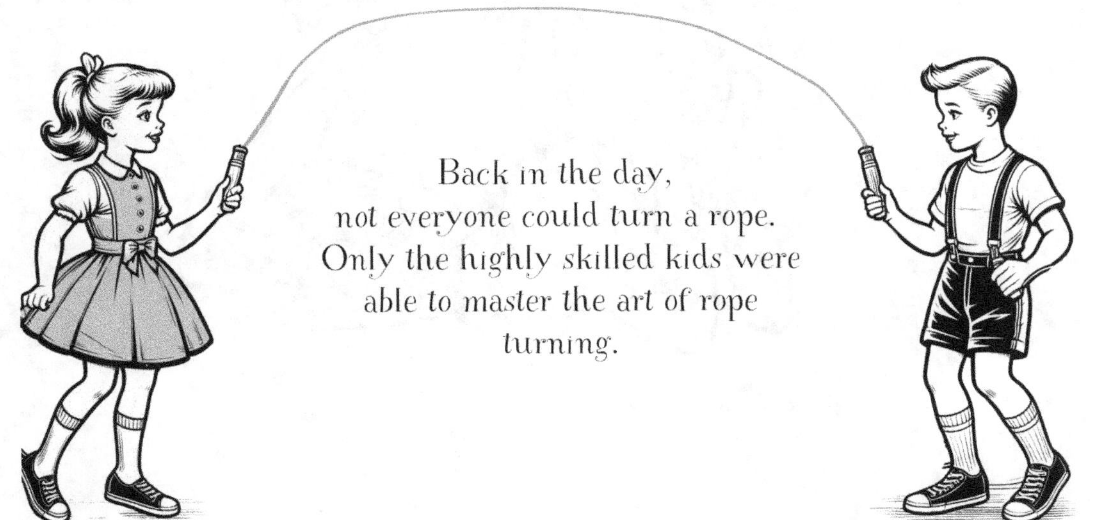

Back in the day,
not everyone could turn a rope.
Only the highly skilled kids were
able to master the art of rope
turning.

69

WILL I MARRY

Have you ever wondered who you'll marry someday? Well, guess what? These skipping rhymes might just hold the answer! They're like a fun game where you skip and rhyme your way to discovering your future sweetheart and their profession, and how many children you will have. These songs are all about playful fun and guessing games, giving kids a peek into their future.

In these rhymes, jumpers call out the alphabet, and the letter that someone misses determines the first letter of your future sweetheart's name or profession. If no one misses, then it's the last letter that counts. So, keep your eyes peeled and your feet moving as you skip along to find out who might be waiting for you in the future!

When Shall I Marry?

A counting game is often played by children to foretell their futures. The jumper asks a question and then counts out a series of answers by saying the rhyme. They keep repeating the rhyme until they reach the last answer. The answer that the jumper misses or the last one they say is the one believed to come true.

When shall I marry?
This year, next year, sometime, never.
 What will I be?
Tinker, tailor, soldier, sailor, rich-man, poor-man, beggar-man, thief.
What will my husband/wife be?
Tinker, tailor, soldier, sailor, rich-man, poor-man, beggar-man, thief.
What will I be?
Lady, baby, gypsy, queen.
What shall I wear?
Silk, satin, cotton, lace
How shall I get it?
Given, borrowed, bought, stolen.
How shall I get to church?
Coach, carriage, wheelbarrow, cart.
Where shall I live?
Big house, little house, pig-sty, barn.

Will I Marry?

Will I Marry, tell me so,
Is the answer yes or no?
Yes, no maybe so,
yes, no, maybe so . . . . .

Ipsey Pipsey

Ipsey Pipsey tell me true,
Ipsey Pipsey tell me true,
Who shall I be married to?
A, B, C. . . . . .

My Young Man

My Young Man,
My young man has gone to France,
To teach the ladies how to dance,
When he comes back,
He'll marry me,
And we'll dance the polka
1 2 3, 1 2 3, 1 2 3,
We'll dance the polka 1 2 3.

Rich Man, Poor Man (1)

Rich man, poor man,
beggar man, thief,
Doctor, lawyer,
Indian Chief.

Her shoes will be
Wood, leather,
high heel, low heel,
sandals, wooden.

Her dress will be made of
Silk, satin, cotton, batten, rags.
Her house will be
Big house, little house, pigpen, barn.
Her rings shall be made of
Diamonds, rubies, emeralds, glass.

How many children will she get?
1, 2, 3 . . . . .
And now you're married you must obey,
You must be true in every way.
You must be kind, you must be good,
And make your husband chop the wood.

Rich Man, Poor Man (2)

This rhyme was traditionally played in England for counting cherry stones, buttons, daisy petals, and other items. It is also commonly played by children in both Britain and America to decide who will be "It" in a game of tag.

Gypsy, Gypsy please tell me,
What my fortune's going to be,
Rich-man, Poor-man, Beggar-man, Thief,
Doc-tor, Law-yer, In-di-an Chief,
Tink-er, Tail-or, Cow-boy, Sail-or.

Carry on saying the rhyme until the person jumping misses a turn and that is the person you will marry.

Would You Marry Me?

A, B, C,... etc.
Say the alphabet until the jumper messes up on a letter.
Name a name that begins with that letter.

(say jumper's name twice) would you come to tea?
Yes, no, maybe so
Skip until someone misses on one of yes/no/maybe

(say jumper's name twice) would you marry me?
Yes, no, maybe so
Skip until someone misses on one of yes/no/maybe

How many children did we have?
1,2,3,4,5,6,..etc.
The number of which someone misses will be the number of their kids.

Bobby Shaftoe

People argue about which Bobby Shafto the song was really about, but evidence shows that it's linked to the Shafto family and was used in politics. Bobby Shafto is believed to be a guy named Robert Shafto, who was a politician in England during the 1700s. The song likely tells the story of how he broke a girl named Bridget's heart by marrying someone else named Anne Duncombe, and Bridget passed away not long after. The song was used by his supporters during the 1761 election. His grandson used it in another election in 1861, and they added more verses to the song around that time.

Bobby Shaftoe went to sea
Silver buckles on his knee
He'll come back to marry me
Bonny Bobby Shaftoe

Bobby Shaftoe's bright and fair
Combing down his yellow hair
He's my love forevermore
Bonny Bobby Shaftoe.

Bobby Shaftoe went to sea
Silver buckles on his knee
He'll come back to marry me
Bonny Bobby shaftoe
How many days until he comes back?
count until someone misses.

SCHOOL RHYMES

These skipping rhymes take us on a journey through the twists and turns of school life, from the funny moments in class to the amusing quirks of our teachers. Whether it's poking fun at tricky math problems, sharing secrets from the classroom, or laughing at the unique characteristics of our favorite educators, these rhymes perfectly capture the essence of the school experience. As we read through these songs, it becomes clear that the feelings and experiences of kids in the past aren't so different from those of kids today.

Dum Dum Dodo

One of the jumpers sings the rhyme, whilst another jumper leaves and selects another person to jump instead of them.

Dum dum dodo
Catch me if you can.
I can run faster
Than (*another jumper's name*) can.
S-C-H-O-O-L spells 'school'
so don't be late.
Jumper runs figure 8 around ends with named jumper following.

Sitting in the Classroom

This song is from New York, Transfiguration Catholic School. It requires 4 players - 2 turners and 2 players take turns jumping:

Sitting in the classroom
chewing bubble gum!

In comes the teacher,
repeat until the 2nd person jumps into the rope.
out goes the gum!

Repeat until the first person jumps out of the rope. Start the song over again until both jumpers mess up, then switch jumpers.

Miss Blackwell

This rhyme starts at a normal speed and then speeds up like a hot pepper as it ends.

Oh no, here comes Miss Blackwell
with her big black stick
Now its time for arithmetic:

One plus one is?
(jumper responds) Two

Two plus two is?
(jumper responds) Four

Four plus four is?
(jumper responds) Eight

Eight plus eight is?
(jumper responds) Sixteen

Now it's time for spelling:
Spell cat.
(jumper responds) C-A-T

Spell dog.
(jumper responds) D-O-G

Spell hot.
(jumper responds) H-O-T

When the jumper finishes spelling HOT swing the rope as fast as possible untill someone misses.

Banana Split

Banana, banana, banana split,
What did you get in arithmetic?
Banana, banana, banana for free,
What did you get in geometry?

Alligator, Alligator

Alligator, alligator
I can't swim.
Call (*say jumper's name*) in.
Jumper enters
Here comes the teacher
With a bamboo stick.
I wonder what I got
in arithmetic.
A, B, C, D, F.

Here Comes the Teacher

Here comes the teacher in our path.
Better get ready for our math.
1 + 1 = 2
2 + 2 = 4
4 + 4 = 8
Now let's spell.... fish
D-O-G spells dog
C-A-T spells cat
O-U-T spells out
Jumper exits

FAMILY, FRIENDS & GOSSIP

Before social media, kids shared their experiences and feelings through skipping rhymes. These songs give us a glimpse into the lives of kids back then. In these rhymes, kids talked about their families, friends, and the juicy gossip swirling around town. It was their own secret space where they could share stories, spill the tea, and have a good laugh together. These rhymes captured the excitement and drama of everyday life. And you know what? Even today, we can still relate to the ups and downs of friendship and family that these rhymes talk about. It's like taking a trip back in time to see that kids back then were just like us!

Down by the Riverside

Down by the riverside
the green grass grows,
Where someone walks,
Some tiptoe, she sings,
She sings so sweet.

She calls over to someone
across the street,
Teacakes, pancakes,
everything you see,
Meet me at the park
at half-past three.

My Mother

My mother and your mother
were hanging up the clothes,
My mother gave your mother
a punch in the nose,
What color was the blood,
Jumper *says color,*
Jumper spells color,
Jumper jumps out,
can say any color.

Miss Mary Mack

Some people think that this song started in the Southern United States, but no evidence was found to support that. Miss Mary Mack was a performer in Ephraim Williams' circus in the 1880s, and the song is possibly referring to her and the elephants she performed with.

Clap along to this song while jumping.

Miss Mary Mack, Mack, Mack
All dressed in black, black, black
With silver buttons, buttons, buttons
All down her back, back, back.
She asked her mother, mother, mother,
For fifteen cents, cents, cents,
To see the elephant, elephant, elephant,
Jump the fence, fence, fence.
He jumped so high, high, high.
He reached the sky, sky, sky,
And he never came back, back, back
Till the Fourth of July, lie, lie.

Bake a Pudding

Bake a pudding.
Bake a pie.
Did you ever
Tell a lie?

Yes, you did.
I know you did.
You broke your mother's
Teapot lid.

I Know a Boy

I know a boy
and he is doubled-jointed,
He gave me an apple
and I was disappointed,
He gave me another
to match the other,

Now, now, Michael
I'll tell your mother,
How many apples
did I eat last night?
1, 2, 3. . . . .

My Best Girl

Jane, Jane,
Replace Jane with a girl's name
With a curl.
Will you jump
As my best girl?
jumper goes in.

Slow at first.
Now that's the way.
On we go
To break of day.

Little Sally Waters

Little Sally Waters
Sitting in a saucer
Crying and weeping
Cause nobody loves her.

Rise Sally, rise Sally.
Turn to the east Sally.
Jumper turns east
Turn to the west Sally.
Jumper turns west
Turn to the one you like the best.
Jumper turns to sweetheart

Dolly Dimple Walks Like This

Dolly Dimple walks like this,
Dolly Dimple talks like this,
Dolly Dimple smiles like this,
Dolly Dimple throws a kiss.

Mary Sittin' on a Gate

Mary, Mary Sittin' on a Gate
Mary, Mary sittin' on a gate,
eating cherries off a plate.
Here comes her mother,
hands her a date.

Grace, Grace Dressed in Lace

Grace, Grace dressed in lace.
Went upstairs to powder her face.
How many boxes did it take?
1, 2, 3, 4, 5,. . .

Old Mother Whittlehouse

Old Mother Whittlehouse,
Had a big fit,
First she did the merry-go-round,
And then she did the split.

Peter Pumpkin

Peter, Peter pumpkin eater,
Peter, Peter pumpkin eater,
Had a wife and couldn't keep her,
Put her in a pumpkin shell,
And there he kept her very well.

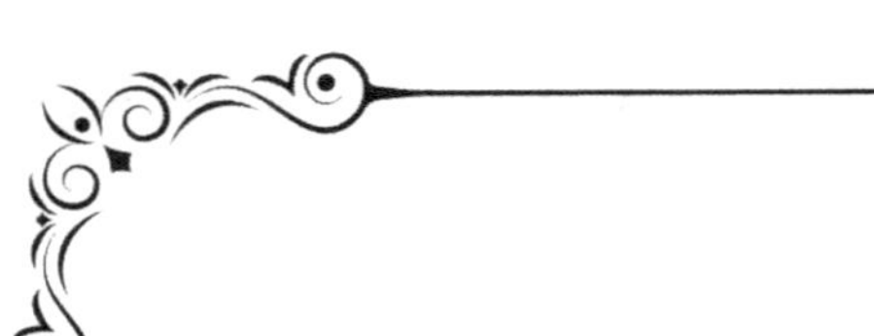

About
Miss Susie had a Steamboat

Warning:
This song includes some rude words and is not suitable for kindergarteners but more for elementary school kids.

This is an American schoolyard rhyme that's very popular among kids, probably because of its cheeky and scandalous words. Each verse leads up to a rude word or profanity which is revealed in the next verse as part of an innocuous word or phrase. Since children are so fond of this rhyme and can be so creative, there are many versions of it.

The song mentions two historic references: 19th-century steamboats, which operated using steam power, and switchboard operators who manually connected telephone calls. These were necessary before modern phones and smartphones.
The origin of the song might be about a famous accident in 1844 when a steamboat named Lucy Walker exploded. Steamboats in the 19th century were not as safe as they are today.

This rhyme shares its tune with another popular jump rope song called "Miss Lucy had a baby," which is why they are often confused with each other. This is probably why some versions of this song are called 'Miss Lucy Had a Steamboat'.

In the old days, anyone who could jump through this rhyme was considered an excellent jumper.

Miss Susie had a Steamboat

Miss Susie had a steamboat,
The steamboat had a bell,
Miss Susie went to heaven,
The steamboat went to...

Hello, operator please
give me number nine,
And if you disconnect me,
I'll kick you from...

Behind the refrigerator,
there was a piece of glass,
Miss Susie sat upon it,
And cut her little...

Ask me no more questions,
Tell me no more lies,
The boys are in the bathroom,
Zipping down their...

Flies are in the city,
The bees are in the park,
Miss Susie and her boyfriend
Are kissing in the D-A-R-K
Dark, dark, dark

D-A-R-K D-A-R-K dark dark dark

The dark is like a movie,
a movie's like a show,
a show is like a TV set
and that's not all

I know I know my ma,
I know I know my pa,
I know I know my sister
with the alligator bra!

Brother's like a sister,
A sister's like an aunt.
An aunt is like a relative
Who likes to rave and rant.

I wish I had a nickel
I wish I had a dime
I wish I had a boyfriend
Who kissed me all the time!

My Ma gave me a nickel
My Pa gave me a dime.
My Sister gave me a boyfriend,
Who'd kiss me all the time

My Ma took back the nickel,
My Pa took back the dime.
My Sister took back her boyfriend,
and gave me Frankenstein!

He made me wash the dishes,
He made me wash the floors,
He made me wash his underwear,
So I kicked him out the door

I kicked him over London,
I kicked him over France.
I kicked him to Hawaii,
where he learned to Hula dance!

My mother's like Godzilla,
My father's like King Kong.
My sister is the stupid one
That taught me this dumb song.

Hello operator,
Please give me number ten.
And if you disconnect me,
I'll sing this song again!

I like coffee (1)

This rhyme is for experienced jumpers.

I like coffee,
I like tea,
I'd like Janey to come in with me.

*Replace "Janey" with the name of
a friend you want to join you in jumping.
That friend runs in while the rope is still
turning. Then that friend calls out the
name of another friend, continuing until
everyone is jumping.*

I like coffee (2)

*Change places this means the left jumper will
switch to be on the right, and the right jumper
will go on the left.*

One jumper says:
I like coffee, I like tea,
I'd like Anne to jump with me.
A second jumper joins.
1, 2, 3 (change places)
4,5,6 (change places),
etc.
Continue until the two jumpers miss.

I like coffee (3)

I like coffee,
I like tea,
I like the boys,
And the boys like me,
Yes, No, Maybe so,
Yes, No, Maybe so . . .

I like coffee (4)

I like coffee
I like coffee, I like tea,
I like 'X name' skipping with me
I don't like coffee, I don't like tea,
(first jumper's name) can skip with (second jumper's name)
So out with me!

I like coffee (5)

I like coffee, I like tea,
I like sitting on daddy's knee,
Salute to the king and bow to the queen,
And turn your back on the gypsy queen.

Little Betty Blue

Little Betty Blue
Lost her shoe.
What shall Betty do?
Buy her another
To match the other
And then she'll walk in two.

When Billy Boy Was One

1 When Billy Boy was o-ne
he learned to suck his thu-umb,
Thumb-dee-ah-dah, thumb-dee-ah-dah,
Half past one, cross down,

2 When Billy boy was two-o,
he learned to tie his shoe-oo,
Two-dee-ah-dah, two-dee-ah dah,
Half past two cross down.

3 When Billy boy was three,
he learned to climb a tree,
Three-dee-ah-dah, three-dee-ah dah,
Half past three cross down.

4 When Billy boy was four,
he learned to shut the door,
Four-dee-ah-dah, four -dee-ah dah,
Half past four cross down.

5 When Billy boy was five,
he learned to jump and dive,
Five-dee-ah-dah, five -dee-ah dah,
Half past five cross down.

6 When Billy boy was six,
he learned to pick up sticks,
Six -dee-ah-dah, six -dee-ah dah,
Half past six cross down.

7 When Billy boy was seven,
he got to heaven,
Seven-dee-ah-dah, seven-dee-ah dah,
Half past seven cross down.

8 When Billy boy was eight,
he learned to clean his plate,
Eight-dee-ah-dah, eight-dee-ah dah,
Half past eight cross down.

9 When Billy boy was nine,
he learned to sing this rhyme,
Nine-dee-ah-dah, nine-dee-ah dah,
Half past nine cross down.

10 When Billy boy was ten,
he learned to say, 'THE END!',
Ten-dee-ah-dah, ten-dee-ah dah,
Half past ten cross down.

When I Was...

When I was **one** I ate a bun,
Going over the sea.
I jumped aboard a sailorman's ship,
And the sailorman said to me,
"Going over, going under,
Stand at attention like a soldier,
With a one, two, and three."

When I was **two** I buckled my shoe,
Going over the sea.
I jumped aboard a sailorman's ship,
And the sailorman said to me, ...

When I was **three** I banged my knee,
When I was **four** I shut the door,
When I was **five** I learned to jive,
When I was **six** I picked up sticks,
When I was **seven** I went to heaven,
When I was **eight** I learned to skate,
When I was **nine** I climbed a vine,
When I was **ten** I caught a hen.

Fortune Teller

Fortune teller,
fortune teller,
please tell me
Who my friend is gonna be…
A,B,C,D…
Go through the abc's until a jumper misses and
think of a name that begins with that letter.

Do Your Duty

These songs serve as sweet reminders of a time before cell phones, when people eagerly awaited the arrival of the mailman, anticipating letters from loved ones or friends. They offer a nostalgic glimpse into the past, brimming with the excitement of waiting for that special letter to arrive.

The songs describe lively scenes from the perspectives of kids, showcasing everyday heroes who play crucial roles in our neighborhoods. Mailmen, policemen, firemen, and doctors are portrayed as symbols of trust, safety, and service. They were respected individuals who took their jobs seriously and worked hard to serve their communities.

Not only do these songs celebrate the dedication of these professions, but they also inject a dash of excitement and adventure into skipping, making it even more enjoyable.

Doctor

Doctor, Doctor, come quick,
Cindy's (*jumper's name*) feeling slightly sick,
Bang on the door one, two, three
We're easy to find you'll see,
There's Cindy, Anne, Julie, Robert and Tim,
There's Cindy, Anne, Julie, Robert and Tim,
Do this again until the jumper misses a name out.

Cobbler, Cobbler

Cobbler, cobbler
Mend my shoe.
Have it done
By half past two.

If half past two
Is far too late,
Have it done
By half past eight.

Fireman, Fireman

Fireman, fireman
Number eight
Hit his head
Against the gate.

The gate flew in.
The gate flew out.
That's the way
He put the fire out.

Early in the Morning

Early in the morning,
about eight o'clock,
What should I hear
but the postman's knock.
Up jumps Margaret
to open the door,
How many letters
did she find on the floor?
A, B, C, D . . . . .

Every morning
at eight o'clock
You all may hear
the postman's knock.
One, two, three, four.
There goes (*jumper's name*)
out the door.
Named jumper exits.

Had a Little Car

Had a little car car,
Two-forty-eight,
Ran around the cor--
Skipper jumps out, runs around one of the turners, and runs back in the rope. Keep saying 'corner' until the skipper jumps back in.
--ner
and slammed on the brakes, but the brakes didn't work,
So I bumped into a lady who bumped into a man,
Who bumped into a police car, man, oh man!
Policeman caught me
Put me on his knee,
Asked me a question
Will you marry me?
Yes, No, Maybe So
repeat until someone misses and that will be the answer.

Had a Little Sportscar

Had a little sportscar,
Went around the cor --
Skipper jumps out and runs around one of the
turners and runs back in the rope. Keep saying
'corner' until the skipper jumps back in.
-- ner
Push my foot on the brakes,
Policeman came and told me off,
How many ales did I drink?
Continue counting until the jumper misses.

Mailman, Mailman, Do Your Duty

Mailman, mailman,
Do your duty
Here comes miss
American Beauty.

She can do the pom-pom
move arms like cheer-leader

she can do the splits,
bend down to touch both toes

but most of all,
she can kiss kiss kiss,
clap hands with a partner

with her red.. hot.. lips.
K - I - S - S
move feet apart further outward with
each letter. The first jumper to fall loses.

Postman, Postman, Do Your Duty (1)

Postman, Postman,
do your duty,
Here comes (*say jumper's name*)
the American beauty,
She can wiggle,
she can waddle,
she can do the splits,
She wears her dresses (*below/above/around*) her hips.
The turners choose which word to sing: below, around or above.

Postman, Postman, Do Your Duty (2)

Postman, Postman,
Do your duty,
Send this letter,
To my cutie,
Don't you stop,
Nor don't delay,
Get it to her,
Right away.

Postman's knock

Postman's knock
Every Morning at 8 o'clock
You can hear the postman's knock
1-2-3-4 there goes (*jumper's name*) out the door
named person jumps out, next in line jumps in

Not Last Night

Not last night
But the night before
Twenty-four salesmen
Knocking at my door.
They ran in.
With books in a bin
They began to shout
As I ran out.
Jumper exits and the next jumper comes in.

Policeman, Policeman, Do Your Duty

Policeman, policeman
Do your duty.
Along comes (*say jumper's name*)
The American beauty.

She can hobble.
She can wobble.
She can do the twist

But I bet she can't do this:
Jump on one foot, one foot.
Jump on one foot
Jump on two feet, two feet.
Jump on both feet
Jump on three feet, three feet.
Jump both feet, hand to the ground
Jump on four feet, four feet.
Jump both feet, hands to the ground.

BUBBLE GUM

Some skipping rhymes are simply about nothing at all! They're filled with silly words that don't really mean anything or minor issues, but they're a blast to sing and jump along to. These rhymes are all about the joy of playing and being with friends, without worrying about making sense. Kids love to make up their own silly verses and add funny gestures to go along with these rhymes. It's all about having fun and letting your imagination run wild while skipping and singing with your friends!

Jump Rope, Jump Rope

Jump rope, jump rope
Will I miss?
Jump rope, jump rope
Just watch this.
Jumper jumps on the rope, stops and freezes.

Five, Ten

Five, ten, fifteen, twenty.
Nobody leaves this rope empty.
If they do, they shall suffer.
Take an end and be a duffer.

Jelly in the Dish

Jelly in the dish,
Jelly in the dish,
Jelly in the dish,

Wiggle-waggle,
Wiggle-waggle,
Jelly in the dish.

Lemon Lime

Lemon and lime
Be on time
Don't be late
Just be on time.
Singing 1, 2
jumper hops out.

3, 4,
The second jumper jumps just 2x & then hops out etc.

5, 6,

Lemon Drops

Lemon drops and sugar candy,
Lemon drops and sugar candy,
Both of these taste just dandy,
Best of all is cherry pop,
How many jumps before I stop?
One, two, three . . . . .

Eeny, Meeny, Miny, Mo

Eeny, meeny, miny, mo,
Catch a rabbit by the toe.
If he hollers, let him go.
Eeny, meeny, miny, mo
My mother told me to
Choose the very best one.

If Bubble Gum is Free

If bubble gum is free, free, free,
Please give some to me, me, me,
I am clever, not a dunce,
How many can I chew at once?
One, two, three . . . .

Ladybug, Ladybug

Ladybug, Ladybug,
turn around,
Ladybug, Ladybug
touch the ground,
Ladybug, Ladybug
shine your shoes,

Ladybug, Ladybug
read the news,
Ladybug, ladybug,
how old are you?
One, two, three, four . . . . .

Zoop La La

Zoop La La,
Zoop La La,
Hey La La,
Zoop La La,
Hey La La,
Zoop, zoop, zoop.

Lady, Lady

Lady, Lady
touch the ground,
Lady, lady,
touch the ground,
Lady, lady,
turn around,
Turn to the east,
and turn to the west,
And choose the one you like the best,

Lady, lady,
touch the ground,
Lady, lady,
turn around,
Lady, lady
show your shoe,
Lady, lady, now skidoo!

One Potato

One potato, two potato,
three potato, four,
Five potato, Six potato,
Seven potato more.
Acha bacha, cucaracha,
out goes Y-O-U

Bubble Gum, Bubble Gum (1)

Bubble gum,
bubble gum,
Penny a packet,
First you chew it,
Then you crack it,
Then you stick it,
In your jacket,
Then your parents,
Kick up a racket.
Bubble gum, bubble gum,
Penny a packet.

Bubble Gum, Bubble Gum (2)

Bubble gum,
bubble gum,
chew and blow,
Jumper blows a bubble
Bubble gum,
bubble gum,
scrape your toe,

Bubble gum,
bubble gum,
tastes so sweet,
Get that bubble gum
off your feet!
Jumper stomps both feet

Bubble Gum, Bubble Gum (3)

Bubble gum, Bubble gum in a dish
How many pieces do you wish?
1..2..3..4..5..

Who Took the Cookie?

Before starting this game, all jumpers take numbers. Numbers can be called in any order.
Jumper singing alone decides whom to call next.

Who took the cookie from the cookie jar?
Turners sing opening verses
Not I took the cookie from the cookie jar.
Then who took the cookie from the cookie jar?

Number 1 took the cookie from the cookie jar.
Jumper 1 enters, sings alone:
Not I took the cookie from the cookie jar.
All jumpers sing this:
Then who took the cookie from the cookie jar?
Jumper 1 sings alone:

Number 2 took the cookie from the cookie jar.
Jumper 2 enters, sings alone:
Not I took the cookie from the cookie jar.
All jumpers sing this:
Then who took the cookie from the cookie jar?
Jumper 2 sings alone:

Number 3 took the cookie from the cookie jar.
Jumper3 enters, sings alone:
Not I took the cookie from the cookie jar.
All jumpers sing this:
Then who took the cookie from the cookie jar?
Continue until all are in.

Butterfly, Butterfly

Butterfly, Butterfly,
throws a kiss, kiss, kiss,
Butterfly, Butterfly, get out
before you miss, miss, miss.

Chimacum, Cheetahs

Chimacum Cheetahs, turn around,
Chimacum Cheetahs, touch the ground,
Chimacum Cheetahs, show your spots,
Chimacum Cheetahs, hot, hot, hot!

Mary

One, two, three A-larry,
One, two, three A-larry,
My first name is Mary,

Don't you think that I look cute?
In my brother's bathing suit?

Sausage in a Pan

Touch the ground,
Turn right round,

Go upstairs,
Say your prayers,
Switch off the light,
And say goodnight!

Sausage in a pan,
Sausage in a pan,

Turn 'em 'over, turn 'em 'over,
Turn around and then turn back once again.
Sausage in a pan.

Pails of Water

Two Little Pails of Water,
Two little Pails of Water,
Two little Pails of Water,

Girls in wooden shoes,
Girls with wooden legs,

You can go through
my garden fence, la, la,
The king drove through
my garden fence, la, la.
One, two, three . . . . .

Whales, Three and More

One whale, two whales,
One whale, two whales,
three whales, four,
One orca, two pods,
three calves, more!

Sugar and Candy

 Amos and Andy,
Sugar and candy
I pop in.
Amos and Andy,
Sugar and candy,
I pop down.
Amos and Andy,
Sugar and candy,
I pop up.
Amos and Andy,
Sugar and candy,
I pop out.

Wash the Dishes

Wash the dishes dry the dishes,
Have a cup of tea.
Don't forget the sugar.
A-one, a-two, a-three . . .

Windy Weather

Windy, Windy Weather,
Windy, Windy Weather,
All in together,
January, February . . . .
Windy, Windy Weather,
They all run out together,
January, February . . . . .

Wire Briar, Limber Lock

Wire briar, limber lock.
Six geese in a flock.
One flew east.
One flew west.
One flew over
The cuckoo's nest.

The Eiffel Tower

The Eiffel Tower,
The Eiffel Tower is
300 meters tall,
From the top to bottom,

We can see the River Seine,
To climb it we pay
One, two, three. . .

Find the Answer

What kind of tradition are skipping ryhmes?

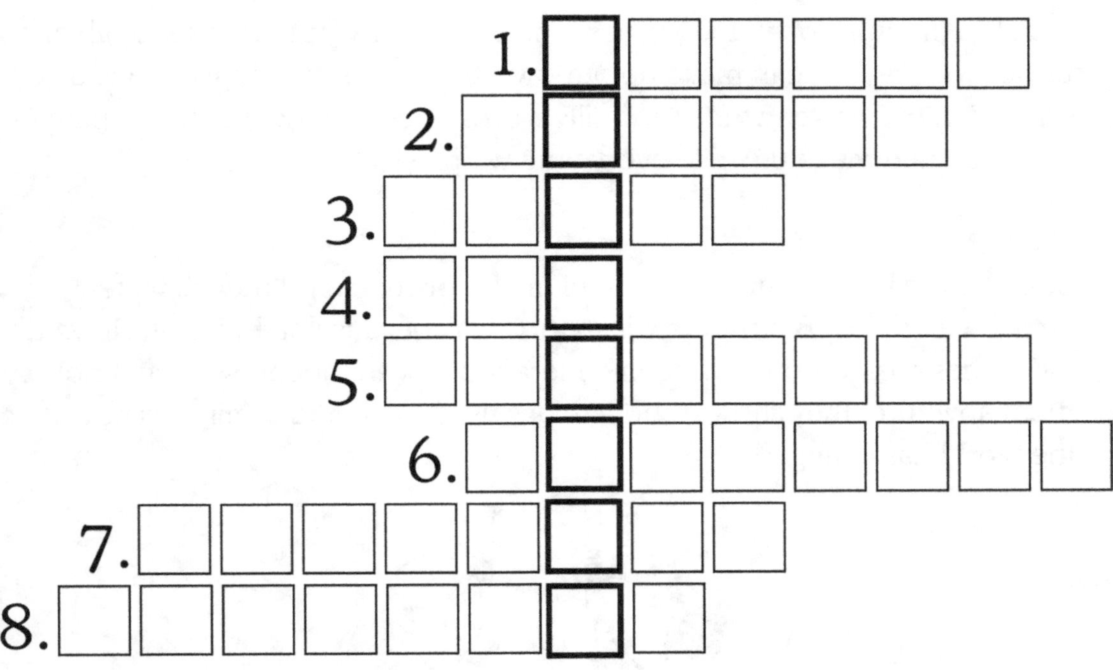

1. I bought it when I went downtown to see Ms. Brown.
2. He broke a bottle and blamed it on me.
3. The queen gave it to her cat.
4. It was small like a nut once.
5. All he could see was the bottom of the sea.
6. He can mend my shoe.
7. Sixteen of them sat on a fence.
8. When she was a baby she used to call "Wah! Wah!".

Funny & Silly

Some of the skipping rhymes are all about silly little moments, like losing a shoe or chasing after a runaway hat. Others take everyday things grown-ups do and turn them into hilarious stories. They're told in a way that only kids understand, with lots of funny jokes and giggles. These funny rhymes make us laugh and help us be creative. We can make up our own silly verses and dance along as we skip. With their catchy tunes and silly words, these rhymes make skipping even more fun and make us smile every time we play!

Note:
Some of the rhymes might seem a bit mean or rude, and they definitely wouldn't be allowed today. But they're still in this book because of their historic value, like old stories passed down through generations. Even though we might not say them anymore, they show us how things used to be and remind us how much the world has changed.

Don't Say 'ain't'

Don't say 'ain't'.
Your mother will faint.
Your father will fall
In a bucket of paint.
Your sister will cry.
Your brother will sigh.
Your dog will call the FBI.

Down in the Alley

Down in the alley
where the garbage grows,
A flea jumped on
an elephant's toes,
The elephant cried
with tears in his eyes,
Why don't you pick on
someone your own size?

Halloweena Heckatee

Halloweena Heckatee
Couldn't brew a cup of tea
The only potion she could brew
Was wishy washy mousetail stew

Nellie Murphy's Got no Drawers

Nellie Murphy's got no drawers
Won't you kindly lend her yours.
For she's going far away
To sing 'Ta ra ra boom de ay.

There She Goes

There she goes, there she goes
Like an elephant on her toes
Look at her feet
She thinks she's neat
Black stockings and dirty feet.

Poor Old Granny

Through every nook and every cranny
The wind blew in on poor old Granny;
Around her knees, into each ear
(And up her nose as well, I fear).

All through the night the wind grew worse,
It nearly made the vicar curse.
The top had fallen off the steeple
Just missing him (and other people).

It blew on man; it blew on beast.
It blew on nun; it blew on priest.
It blew the wig off Auntie Fanny--
But most of all, it blew on Granny!!

Five Little Monkeys

Five little monkeys jumping on the bed,
One fell off and bumped her head,
Mama called the doctor and the doctor said,
"No more monkeys jumping on the bed!"

Four little monkeys jumping on the bed,
One fell off and bumped his head,
Mama called the doctor and the doctor said,
"No more monkeys jumping on the bed!"

Three little monkeys jumping on the bed,
One fell off and bumped her head,
Mama called the doctor and the doctor said,
"No more monkeys jumping on the bed!"

Two little monkeys jumping on the bed,
One fell off and bumped his head,
Mama called the doctor and the doctor said,
"No more monkeys jumping on the bed!"

One little monkey jumping on the bed,
He fell off and bumped his head,
Mama called the doctor
and the doctor said,
"Put those monkeys to bed!"

No little monkeys jumping on the bed,
None fell off and bumped their head,
Mama called the doctor and the doctor said,
"Put those monkeys back in bed!

A Sailor Went to Sea

A Sailor went to sea, sea, sea.
To see what he could see, see, see.
But all that he could see, see, see
Was the bottom on the sea, sea, sea.

My Mommy Told Me

My mommy told me,
If I was good-y
She would buy me,
A rubber dolly.

My auntie told her,
I met a soldier.
Now she won't buy me,
A rubber dolly.

I went upstairs
to make my bed,
I made a mistake
and bumped my head.

I went downstairs
to milk my cow,
I made a mistake
and milked the sow.

I went into the kitchen
to bake a pie,
I made a mistake
and baked a fly.

How many flies does it take
to make a pie?
1, 2, 3, 4, 5, etc.

*Count until someone misses the rope
and that will be the answer.*

3 Blind Mice

A horse, a flea, and three blind mice,
Sat on a curbstone shooting dice,
The horse, he slipped and fell on his head,
"Well that was silly," the others said.

15 Cents

I asked my parents for 15 cents,
To see the platypus jump the fence,
She jumped so high she touched the sky,
And didn't come back till
the Fourth of July.

I See London, I See France

I see London,
I see France,
I see (*say jumper's name*) pants,

Not too big,
Not too small,
Just the size of cannonballs!

Hurry Scurry

Hurry Scurry had a worry
No one liked his chicken curry
Stuck his finger in the pot
Chicken curry way too hot

I Know a Little Lady

I know a little lady,
But her name is Miss,
She went around the corner,
To buy some fish,
She met a little fellow,
And she gave him a dish,
I know a little lady,
But her name is Miss.

Three, Six, Nine

Three, Six, Nine,
Three, Six,Nine,
the goose drank wine,
The monkey chewed tobacco
on the street car line,
The lion choked,
the monkey croaked,
And they all went to heaven
in a little row boat,
Clap-Clap! Clap-Clap!

Dancing Dolly

Dancing Dolly has no sense.
Bought a fiddle for eighteen cents.
But the only tune that she could play
Was (*jumper's name*) get out
of the donkey's way.
Named jumper exits.

Ali Baba

Ali Baba and the forty thieves
went to school with dirty knees.
The teacher said, "Stand at ease".
Ali Baba and forty thieves.

Chocolate Bears

Chocolate bears and gingerbread cats,
All dressed up in whipped-cream hats.
Danced in the garden under the moon,
Beat sweet rhythms with a wooden spoon,
Whirling, turning, jumping to the beat,
Melting down to their ice cream feet.

When the baker ran to see,
They ran beneath the gum-gum tree,
Running in between the rows,
Tripping over ice cream toes.
There were 1, 2, 3 . . .

Anthy Maria

Anthy Maria jumped
near the fire,
The fire too hot,
she jumped in the pot,
The pot was too black,
she jumped in a crack,
The pot was soon over,
she jumped in some clover,

Clover's too sweet;
she kicked up her feet,
Feet was soon over,
she cried 1, 2, 3,
Jumped in a tree,
The tree was so high
she couldn't go higher,
Long came a breeze, blew her away.

50 Cents

I asked my mother for fifty cents
To see the elephant jump the fence.
He jumped so high he touched the sky,
And never came back till
the Fourth of July.

I Had a Dolly

I had a dolly dressed in green.
I didn't like her.
I gave her to the queen.
The queen didn't like her.
She gave her to the cat.
The cat didn't like her
Because she wasn't fat.

Fuzzy Wuzzy

The origin of the term "Fuzzy Wuzzy" in this song is not quit clear. British soldiers in the late 1800s called the Hadendoa warriors from Sudan "Fuzzy Wuzzies" because of their unique hair that looked like fuzz to them. Besides that, there's also a "Fuzzy Wuzzy math formula" linked to "Lanchester's Law." This formula shows that in battles, adding just one soldier increases the group's strength by more than the strength of just one extra soldier. It's like their teamwork multiplies their power. But, this song isn't really about history or math. It's just a playful tune with catchy, funny words that kids love to skip to. It is also a tongue twister, making it extra difficult to sing and jump at the same time.

Fuzzy Wuzzy was a bear
Fuzzy Wuzzy had no hair
Fuzzy Wuzzy wasn't fuzzy
No, by gosh, he wasn't, was he?

Silly Willy was a worm
Silly Willy wouldn't squirm
Silly Willy wasn't silly
No, by gosh, he wasn't really

Iddy Biddy was a mouse
Iddy Biddy had no spouse
Iddy Biddy wasn't pretty
Oh, by gosh, it was a pity

Fuzzy Wuzzy was a bear
Fuzzy Wuzzy had no hair
Fuzzy Wuzzy wasn't fuzzy
No, by god, he wasn't, was he?

Eleanor

Eleanor, where are you going?
"Upstairs to take a bath,"
Eleanor, with legs like toothpicks,
And a long neck like a giraffe,
Eleanor got in the bathtub,
Eleanor pulled out the plug,
Oh my goodness,
Oh my soul,
Eleanor nearly floats down the hole.

Hanky Panky

Down by the banks
of the hanky panky,
where the bullfrogs jump
from bank to bank,
saying eeps ipes oops umps
chilly willy ding dong,
I pledge allegiance to the flag,
Michael Jackson makes me gag,
Coca Cola drink it up
now we're talking Seven Up,
Seven Up has no caffeine.
Now we're talking Billy Jean
Billy Jean is out of sight.

now we're talking dynamite,
dynamite blew up the school,
now we're talking really cool,
really cool is really neat,
now we're talking stinky feet,
10, 9, 8, 7, 6, 5, 4, 3, 2, 1.

I Know Something

I know something,
But I won't tell,
Three little monkeys,
In a peanut shell,
One can read,
And one can dance,
And one has a hole,
In the seat of his pants!

I Went Downtown

I went downtown
To see Ms. Brown,
She gave me a nickel
To buy a pickle,
The pickle was sour,
So I bought a flower.

The flower was dead,
she gave me a tack.
The tack was sharp,
she gave me a harp.

The harp was broken,
she gave me a cloak.

The cloak was tight,
she gave me a kite.
The kite away flew,
and I did too.
The jumper runs out at too.

In the Dark World

In the dark, dark world
There's a dark, dark country.
In the dark, dark country
There's a dark, dark wood.
In the dark, dark wood
There's a dark, dark house.
In the dark, dark house
There's a man trying to mend a fuse.

Blackbirds, Blackbirds

Blackbirds, blackbirds,
Sitting on a wire,
What do you do there?
May we ask?
We just sit to see the day,
Then we flock and fly away.
By 1, 2, 3. . . . .

Birdie, Birdie in the Sky

Birdie, birdie in the sky,
Why'd ya do that in my eye?
Birdie, birdie in the sky,
Gee, I'm glad that cows don't fly.

Engine, Engine Number Nine

One jumper points to another jumper and sings:

Engine, engine number nine,
Running down the Chicago line,
If the train should jump the track,
Do you want your money back?
(Y-E-S or N-O)

The jumper you're pointing at when you say "back" answers either "yes" or "no".
You then spell the answer: y-e-s spells yes and you now leave or n-o spells no and you now leave.

I Can Do a Polka

I can do a polka,
I can do a split,
I can do a tap dance,
just like this!
1, 2, 3 . . . .

Noble Knight, Noble Knight

Noble Knight, Noble Knight
Try, try, try with all of your might
Follow the rules
And you'll be cool!
Noble Knight, Noble Knight

Anna Banana

Anna Banana
Plays the piano.
All she can play
Is, "The Star Spangled Banner".
Anna, Banana Split!

Jingle Bells

Jingle bells,
Batman smells,
Robin laid an egg.
The Batmobile lost a wheel
And Joker took ballet.

Ladies and Gentlemen

Ladies and gentlemen
Children too,
This young lady's
Going to boogie for you.

She's going to turn around.
Jumper turn around.
She's going to touch the ground.
Jumper touch ground.

She's going to
shimmy, shimmy, shimmy
Jumper wiggles hips.
Till her drawers fall down.

She never went to college.
She never went to school.
But when she came back,
She was a nasty fool.

TIP 

Common Mistakes to Avoid

1. **Coordination is Key:** Make sure everyone is in sync with each other. Mistiming jumps or rope swings can lead to accidents.
2. **Clear Communication:** Establish clear signals or cues between the swingers and jumpers to ensure smooth transitions and avoid collisions.
3. **Maintain Proper Spacing:** Keep a safe distance between jumpers to prevent entanglements and ensure each person has enough room to maneuver.
4. **Watch Your Surroundings:** Be aware of obstacles or hazards in the area where you're skipping to avoid tripping or getting tangled in the rope.
5. **Practice Patience:** Take your time to learn and coordinate movements together as a group. Rushing can lead to mistakes and accidents.

ACTION RHYMES

Some skipping rhymes include fun actions like touching your heel, doing a split, or even jumping with your eyes closed. These actions make skipping even more exciting and challenging, perfect for advanced jumpers! The lyrics of the song will indicate which actions to perform while jumping, so pay close attention and get ready to stretch, jump, and move along with these action-packed rhymes!

Some songs involve doing the splits. In the skipping rhymes world, doing the "splits" means spreading your legs wide apart to form a big V shape, unless you're flexible enough to do the full split.

Queen Bee

This is a mix of jump rope, tag, and follow the leader.
Anything the Queen bee does, the worker bee must copy while trying to catch up with and tag
the Queen bee. The Queen may leave and enter the rope they wish.

Queen bee follow me,
See if you can catch me.

Hippopotamus

Do each of the commands while skipping.

Spelling Hipp-o-pot-a-mus
You've got the hip
Put your hand on your hip
The "O"
Put arms up in the air in the shape of an O.
The "Pot"
Put arms in front of you, still in the O shape, imagine you're
hugging a big pot in front of you.
The "Toe"
Lift one of your legs up and touch your toe with your hand.
And the "Miss"!
Stop the skipping rope by jumping over it, one leg on each side,
when it's on the ground.

Miss Brown

I went downtown,
to see Miss Brown,
She gave me a nickel,
to buy a pickle,
The pickle was sour
so she gave me a flower,
The flower was black
so she gave me a smack,
The smack was hard
so she gave me a card,
And on the card it said:

Little Spanish dancer
turn around
turn while jumping
Little Spanish dancer,
touch the ground
touch ground
Little Spanish dancer
tie your shoe
jump on one leg, pretend to tie your shoe.
Little Spanish dancer,
sixty-four skidoo
jumper exits.

Spanish Dancer

Spanish dancer, do the split,
Spanish dancer, give a kick,
Spanish dancer clicks a shoe,
Spanish dancer chooses YOU!

Spanish dancer, turn around,
Spanish dancer, get out of town.
Spanish dancer, skit skat, skidoo.

We Like

We like (*name a jumper*)
She is sweet,
She jumps rope
With both her feet.
She jumps high
On all her toes
She gives a hop &
OUT she goes
Jumper exits and the next jumper comes in.

Oliver

Oliver jump
Oliver jump jump jump,
Oliver kick
Oliver kick kick kick,
Oliver twist
Oliver twist twist twist,
Oliver ski
Oliver ski ski ski,
Oliver straddle
Oliver straddle straddle straddle,
Oliver twist
Oliver twist twist twist.

Miss Sue from Alabama

Miss Sue, Miss Sue,
Snap fingers.
Miss Sue from Alabama.

Sitting in her rocker,
Eating Betty Crocker,
Pretend to eat.

Watching the clock go
Tick-tock, tick-tock
banana rock.
Point index fingers up and then tick.

Tick-tock, tick-tock
banana rock,
tock from left to right.

A B C D E F G,
Wash those spots right off of me.
Brush hands-off shoulders.

Oosha mama, oosha mama,
Point fingers and dance.
Oosha mama, FREEZE!
Freeze and don't move!

When Pebbles Was a Baby

This is an old Florida rhyme. Jumper should mimic the actions of each stage.

When Pebbles was a baby, a baby, a baby
When Pebbles was a baby, she used to go like this:
"Wah! Wah!"
mime crying

When Pebbles was a toddler, a toddler, a toddler
When Pebbles was a toddler she used to go like this:
"Wah! Wah!"
"Give me a Sucker"
mimes licking lollipop

When Pebbles was a kid, a kid, a kid
When Pebbles was a kid she used to go like this:
"Wah! Wah!"
"give me a sucker"
"I know the answer!"
waves hand in the air

When Pebbles was a teenager, a teenager, a teenager
When Pebbles was a teenager she used to go like this:
"Wah! Wah!"
"Give me a sucker"
"I know the answer"
"Ohh! Ah! I lost my bra! I must have left it on my bed!!!"
cover chest

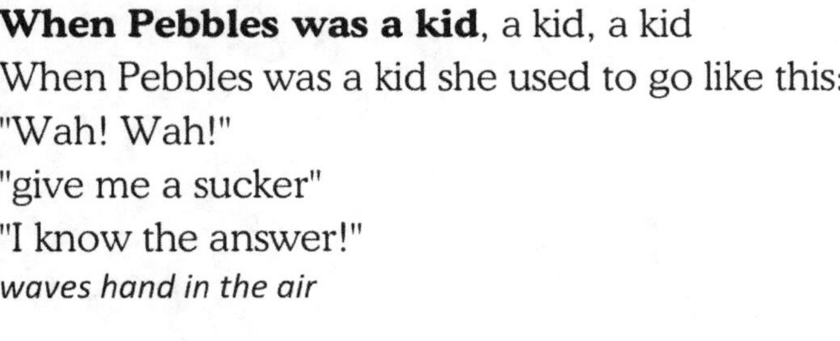

When Pebbles was a mother, a mother, a mother
When Pebbles was a mother she used to go like this:
"Wah! Wah!"
"Give me a sucker"
"I know the answer"
"Ohh! Ah! I lost my bra! I must have left it on my bed!!!"
"Ding Dong Dinner's ready!"
mime pulling bell

When Pebbles was a grandma, a grandma, a grandma
When Pebbles was a grandma she used to go like this:
"Wah! Wah!"
"Give me a sucker"
"I know the answer"
"Ohh! Ah! I lost my bra! I must have left it on my bed!!!"
"Ding Dong Dinner's ready!"
"Oh! my aching back!"
bend over

When Pebbles was in heaven, in heaven, in heaven
When Pebbles was in heaven, she used to like this:
"Wah! Wah!"
"Give me a sucker"
"I know the answer"
"Ohh! Ah! I lost my bra! I must have left it on my bed!!!"
"Ding Dong Dinner's ready!"
"Oh! my aching back!"
"Alleluia!"
throw arms up

With actions to accompany each line, these versions of Texaco Mexico are for more advanced jumpers.

Texaco Mexico (1)

Texaco Mexico
Turners turn rope

Went over the hill
Jumper jumps into the moving rope

Where far away
Jumper jumps

And they do some splits, splits, splits
Jumper executes splits

And they turn around round round
Jumper turns around

And they touch the ground, ground, ground
Jumper touches the ground

And they do some kicks, kicks, kicks
Jumper does kicks

And they pay their taxes, taxes, taxes
Jumper slaps the hand of the turner

And they get outa town, town, town
Jumper moves out of the rope

And they jump back in, in, in
Jumper jumps back into the rope

And that's the end, end, end
Jumper jumps out of the rope.

Texaco Mexico (2)

TEXICO Texico, Texico,
Over the hills to Mexico,
*on the word "over" the rope begins
going all the way around and continues
doing this until the end of the rhyme.*
Where the Spanish dancers
do the kicks, the kicks,
do kicks
Where the Spanish dancers
do the splits, the splits,
jump with legs apart

Where the Spanish dancers
twirl around, around,
twirl around
Where the Spanish dancers
jump up and down, up and down,
jump high
Where the Spanish dancers
get out of town.
jump out of the rope.

Texaco Mexico (3)

Texico, Mexico all the way to Texico
swinging rope on the ground

where they do the splits, splits, splits
spread legs as if to do splits

and high heel kicks, kicks, kicks
bend knees

and turn around, round, round,
spin

and touch the ground, ground, ground
bend down and touch the ground with your fingers

and they eat red hot chili peppers
spin the rope quickly.

Jack be Nimble

This rhyme was first found in 1815, it combined fortune-telling with sport. The challenge was to jump over a candlestick without putting out the flame, which was believed to bring good luck. However, it's crucial for safety not to attempt this at home.

This is a double-dutch jump rope song. One jumper at a time. And depending on how good the jumper is, will normally be followed by another song until the jumper misses.

Jack be nimble
Jack be quick
Jack jumped over the candlestick.

Jack jumped high,
Jack jumped low,
Jack jumped over
and burned his toe!

Jumper pops up very high with both feet leaving the ground at the same time.
mumble
Put both feet together making very small hops
kick
repeatedly kick one foot outward and back again
sizzler
cross and uncrossing feet and legs
split
Open and close legs about 5 feet apart
pop-ups
Jump high in the rope with both feet coming off the ground together
10 to 1, hit it!
10, 9, 8, 7, 6, 5, 4, 3, 2, 1.

I'm a Little Dutch Girl

I'm a little Dutch girl
Dressed in blue.
Here are the things
I like to do:

Salute to the captain,
Bow to the queen,
mimic a bow
Turn by back
turn around and face the other direction
On the submarine.

I can do the tap dance,
do a dance
I can do the split,
jump up high with legs apart
I can do the holka polka
turn around
Just like this.

Little White Rabbit

Little white rabbit,
Hop on one foot, one foot.
Little white rabbit,
Hop on two feet, two feet.
Little white rabbit,
Hop on three feet, three feet.
The jumper puts one hand on the ground.
Little white rabbit,
Hop on no feet, no feet.
The jumper runs out.

Soda Pop

Soda pop, Soda pop
Sierra Mist
Can you do do this with a twist?
Jumper performs these actions
Number 1: touch your nose
Number 2: touch your shoe.
Number 3: bend your knee.
Number 4: touch the floor.
Number 5: wave goodbye.
Jumper exits and next jumper comes in.

Teddy Bear

Teddy Bear, Teddy Bear
Jump up & down
Jumper jumps up and down
Teddy Bear, Teddy Bear
Turn around
Jumper turns around
Teddy Bear, Teddy Bear,
Touch the ground
Jumper touches the ground
Teddy Bear, Teddy Bear,
Get out of town
Jumper exits and the next jumper comes in

Boogie Woogie

Ladies and gentlemen,
children too,
This young kid's
Gonna boogie for you!
See him KICK his feet!
Jumper kicks

See him TWIST to the beat!
Jumper does the twist

See him get so LOW.
Jumper gets low

See him touch his TOE.
Jumper touches toe

See him shimmy, shimmy, shake
Jumper wiggles hips

'Till no more jumps can he take.
Jumper exits and next jumper comes in

California Oranges

California oranges,
50 cents a pack,
California oranges,
tap me on the back!
*A second jumper comes in and tags the first, who leaves,
then repeat the song*

Here I Go!

I run in and around I go.
Clap my hands and nod just so.
Jumper claps hands and nods

I lift my knee and touch my toe.
Jumper lifts knee and touches toe

I give a shout,
Jumper gives a shout

Then I go OUT.
Jumper exits and next jumper comes in.

Hand Jives

Hello, Hello, gramma,
gramma sick in bed
called the doctor
this is what he said,
Let's get the rhythm
of the head "ding dong,"
Shake head left to right.

Let's get the rhythm of the hands,
clap hands twice.

Let's get the rhythm of the feet,
stamp feet twice.

Let's get the rhythm of the "hot dog,"
while saying "hot dog" rotate hips with hands on them.

Now put it all together and what have you got "ding, dong,"
clap hands, stamp feet,

"hot dog"

Now put it all back and what have you got "hot dog,"
stamp feet, clap hands,

"ding dong".

Teddy Bear

Dozens of variations of this chant have been recorded in the last century, but this is by far the most popular one since 1920. If you really want to make others watch your smooth jump rope skills, this is the go-to rhyme. Mimic the actions mentioned in Teddy Bear, Teddy Bear for an extra challenge.

Teddy bear, teddy bear, dressed in blue,
Can you do what I tell you to?
Teddy bear, teddy bear, turn around.
Jumper turns around
Teddy bear, teddy bear, touch the ground.
Jumper touches the ground
Teddy bear, teddy bear, do the splits.
Jumper does the split
Teddy bear, teddy bear, give a high kick.
Jumper kicks the air
Teddy bear, teddy bear, go upstairs.
Jumper pantomimes going upstairs
Teddy bear, teddy bear, say your prayers.
Jumper folds hands as if praying
Teddy bear, teddy bear, Brush your hair.
Jumper pantomimes brushing hair
Teddy bear, teddy bear, turn out the light.
Jumper pantomimes turning out light switch
Teddy bear, teddy bear, say good night.
G-O-O-D-N-I-G-H-T.
Spell on each jump.

Under and Over the Moon

Under
The player runs under the rope as it turns and runs around the end holder.

and over
The player jumps over the rope from the opposite side

Under and over the moon

The baby dropped the spoon

So pick it up
another player reaches down and pretends to pick up the spoon

Pick it up
they do it again.

Under and over the moon!

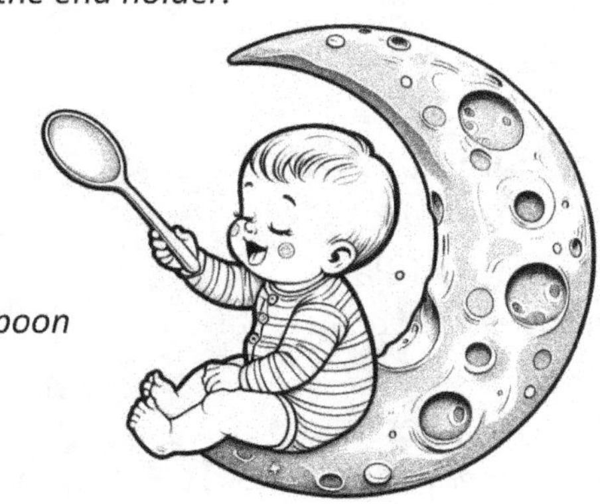

Back to back

Back to back
jumpers turn to jump back to back

Face to face
jumpers turn to jump face to face

Shake your partner's hand
jumpers shake hands

And change your place
jumpers repeat

Two Little Bluebirds

Two little bluebirds
two jumpers jump
Sitting on a wall.

One named Peter.
First *jumper takes a bow*
One named Paul.
Second *jumper takes a bow*

Fly away, Peter.
First *jumper exits*
Fly away, Paul.
Second *jumper exits*

don't come back
until your birthday's called
January, February.....
each jumper returns on their birthday month

Come back, Peter.
First *jumper re-enters*
Come back, Paul.
Second *jumper re-enters.*

Two Little Sausages

Two little sausages
frying in the pan
two jumpers skip together
One went POP
and the other went BANG!
One jumps out one side, the other skipper on the other side.

History & Politics

Skipping rhymes about politics and historic events are like little windows into the past, giving us glimpses of what life was like during different times. These rhymes often mention famous figures or important events, but in a fun and playful way that makes them easy to remember. They might include references to presidents, wars, or other significant moments in history, turning them into catchy tunes that kids can chant while they skip rope. While some of the references might be too complex for younger children to fully understand, they can still enjoy the rhythm and melody of the rhymes, and they might even learn a little something about history along the way.

Christopher Columbus

Christopher Columbus,
Sailed the ocean blue,
In fourteen hundred,
And ninety-two.

Christopher Columbus
Was a very brave man.
He sailed the ocean
In an old tin can.

Charlie Chaplin Went to France

Charlie Chaplin was a famous actor and comedian known for his silent films in the early 20th century. He mastered the art of pantomime, using exaggerated gestures and facial expressions to tell stories and entertain audiences. With his bowler hat, mustache, and funny walk, he made people all around the world laugh without saying a word!

This skipping rhyme has movements that copy Chaplin's funny way of acting. This is an Australian version, from the Salisbury Primary School in Brisbane, Australia in the mid 1950s.

Charlie Chaplin went to France,
To teach the ladies the hula dance,
First he did the Rumba,
Then he did the twist,
Then he did the Highland Fling,
And then he did the splits.

These songs came about when women were fighting for their right to vote. They celebrate their struggle to be able to vote just like men.

Vote, Vote (1)

Vote, vote, for *(say a jumper's name)*,
Calling *(say next jumper's name)* at the door.
Patsy is the one who makes all the fun,
So we don't need Elsie any more,
Shut the door.

Elsie has to skip out and Patsy skips in without missing a skip.

Vote Vote (2)

Vote vote vote for dear *(jumper's name)*
Who's that knocking at your door?
Well if it's *(jumper's name)*
jumper calls out a name and that person jumps in
Let her in and we'll sock her on the chin,
And we won't vote for *(jumper's name)* anymore,
Two, four, shut the door, get out
The first jumper gets out.
Repeat with the name of the jumper that went out.

Lizzie Borden

Lizzie Borden was an American woman who was accused of a serious crime. She went to trial in 1892 and was found not guilty. This rhyme became famous during her trial. Even though she didn't like people talking about her and even though she was found not guilty, kids would still follow her around and sing the rhyme. The original words of the rhyme were changed to keep the song kid-friendly.

Lizzie Borden took a stick
She gave her mom forty tricks,
After she saw what she had done,
She gave her dad forty-one.
Lizzie Borden got away,
For her crime she did not pay.

Waterloo

At the battle of Waterloo
This is what the soldiers do:
Left, right, left, right
Jumps on the correct foot
All the way to Timbuktu.

Lincoln, Lincoln

Lincoln, Lincoln,
I been thinking
What the heck
Have you been drinking?
Looks like water
Tastes like wine
Oh my gosh, its turpentine

I had a little bird

This rhyme plays around with the word "influenza" (the flu) and was popular during the 1918 flu pandemic.

I had a little bird,
And its name was Enza.
I opened the window
And in-flew-enza.

Keep it Boiling

During a period called the Emergency in Dublin, Ireland, in the year 1939, inspectors known as "Glimmer men" were visiting private homes. They were responsible for enforcing restrictions on the use of coal gas during specific hours.

Keep it boiling
on the glimmer,
if you don't
you get no dinner.

I won't Go to Casey's Any More

This song originated during the Prohibition era in the USA, when the use of alcoholic beverages was banned.

No, I won't go to Casey's
any more, more, more,
There's a big fat policeman
by the door, door, door.
He grabs you by the collar,
And makes you pay a dollar.
No, I won't go to Casey's any more.

George Washington

George Washington,
Never told a lie,
Till he ran around the cor --
Skipper jumps out, runs around one of the turners, and runs back in the rope. Keep saying
'corner' until the skipper jumps back in.

-- ner
Stole a cherry pie,
Jumper re-enters
How many cherries were in that pie?
Hot peppers!
Calls fast turning
1, 2, 3, 4....
Carry on counting until the person jumping misses.

The White House

Landon in the White House,
Landon in the White House,
Waiting to be elected,

Rosevelt in the garbage can,
Waiting to be collected.

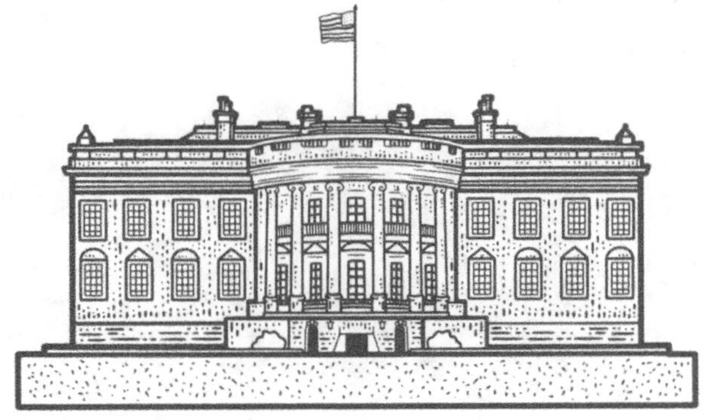

Charlie Chaplin

This song originated around 1930.

Charlie Chaplin came to Duluth
To have a dentist pull his tooth.
First he hollered then he yelled
Then he pulled the emergency bell.

Charlie Chaplin has big feet.
Thinks he owns the whole darn street.
If that street were made of glass
Charlie would fall and break his ---
Don't get excited. Don't get alarmed.
Charlie would fall and break his ARM!

Charlie Chaplin went to France
To teach the ladies how to dance.

Charlie Chaplin washing up
Broke a saucer and a cup.

Charlie Chaplin went to war.
When he came back
His pants were tore.

I Had a Little Puppy

There are many variations to this song, in some of them the puppy is replaced with a baby. The most famous version is called 'Miss Lucy had a baby'. The meaning of this rhyme has evolved over time. The earliest versions were a bit rude and included political or dark humor. However, as the years passed, changes were made to the lyrics to make it more appropriate for children's play. The result of these changes is a silly, imaginative rhyme that doesn't carry a deeper meaning.

The name 'Tiny Tim' could be inspired by the 'Tiny Tim" comic strip section that was popular during the Depression-era, or by the character from Charles Dickens' book called "A Christmas Carol". The lady with the alligator purse represents authority or wealth, likely because an alligator purse was seen as a luxury item. Her role in the rhyme is to add humor to the story; she disagrees with the doctor and the nurse about the seriousness of the puppy's illness, offering a less serious diagnosis (hiccups).

I had a little puppy.
His name was Tiny Tim.
I put him in the bathtub,
To see if he could swim.

He drank up all the water.
He ate a bar of soap.
The next thing you know,
He had a bubble in his throat.

In came the doctor,
second jumper comes in.
In came the nurse,
third jumper comes in.
In came the lady,
With the alligator purse.
fourth jumper comes in.

Mumps said the doctor,
Measles said the nurse,
Hiccups said the lady,
With the alligator purse,

Out went the doctor,
second jumper comes out.
Out went the nurse,
third jumper comes out.
Out went the lady
With the alligator purse
fourth jumper comes out.

Amy Johnson Flew in an Airplane

This song came from Britain, around 1930. Amy Johnson was a pioneering English aviator who became the first woman to fly solo from London to Australia in 1930, and her achievements have inspired numerous tributes in music, literature, and popular culture. This song is one of them.

Amy Johnson flew in an airplane.
Away to America
and never came back again.
She flew in an old tin lizzy
Enough to make you dizzy.
Amy Johnson in an airplane.

The End

YOUR REVIEW IS MY SUPERPOWER!

Loved this book?
Help others find it!
Write a review and
share the magic!

For comments, questions, or just to say hi,
contact us at: info@nona-books.com

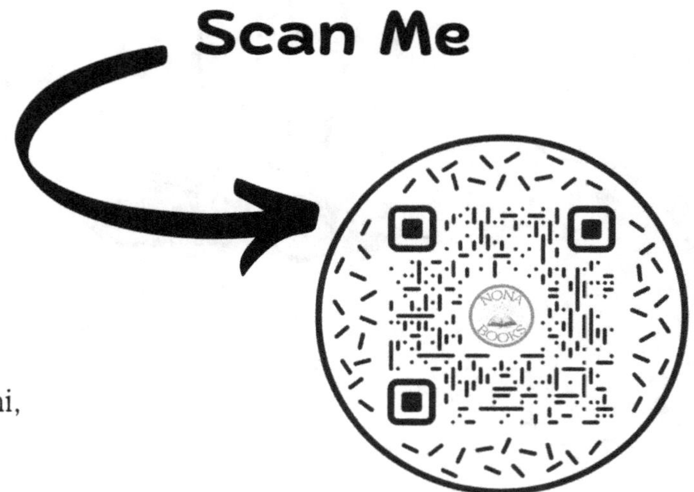

MEET THE AUTHOR

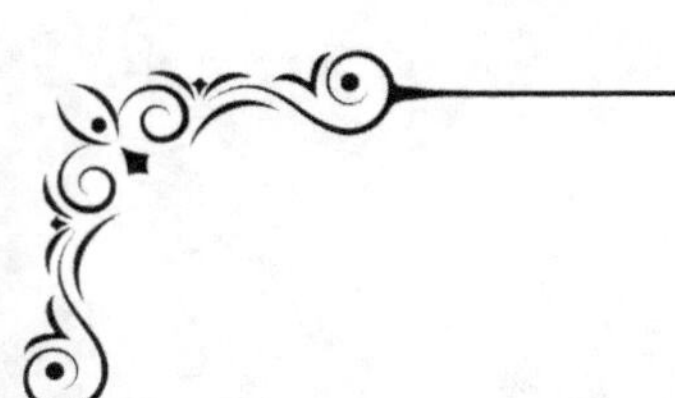

I grew up in a family that didn't have a lot of money. My parents were always working hard to put food on the table, so they didn't have much free time to play with me and my 3 siblings. We didn't have any money for books or toys, either.

I Was a Real Bookworm
But that's okay, because I found my best friends at the library! I loved to read so much, that I practically lived there. I was a real bookworm. My favorite book was "Little House on the Prairie". I read it 7 times! I wished I could live on a farm with Laura Ingalls and her family. I loved their small-town stories and how they always stuck together, and I loved to hate Nellie Oleson. That book really shaped me as a grown-up.

The Girl Who Didn't Know Things
We didn't talk about much at home, and reading Encyclopedia was boring, so I didn't know a lot of things. At school, or with friends, I always felt like the one who knew the least. Everyone else seemed to know things about the world that surrounds us, and it made me feel insecure, stupid, and like I was less than the others.

My Passion Today
Today, I'm a mom to 4 amazing boys who, like me, love getting lost in a good book. I write non-fiction children's books because I want them, and all kids, to learn cool things and feel good about themselves.

My Biggest Challenge

My biggest challenge in writing books is making sure they are interesting enough to keep kids reading. I want them to feel that reading is not a chore, but an adventure - just like my trips to the library were for me! The words, the illustrations, and the photos in my books are all there to make reading fun and keep young readers turning the pages. Nothing gives me a greater joy than a kid with their nose stuck in a book.

You Should Know That...

You're important and amazing just the way you are. You can overcome anything, just believe in yourself.

I hope that you enjoy my books and start your own amazing adventures of becoming the best that you can be!

Love,
Iris.

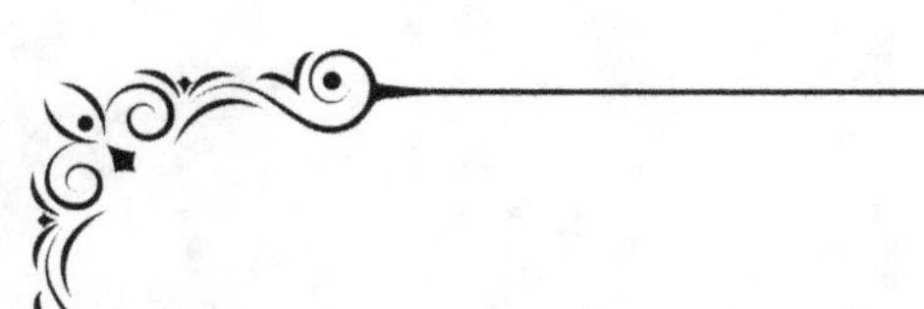

Don't Lose Hop!
The Fun Doesn't Stop!

The rhymes are done,
the jumps are through,
But more jump rope fun
can come to you!
Just send an email,
it's quick and it's neat,
Get jump rope games,
a skippy treat!

For jump rope fun that never ends,
Send us a note and we'll be your jump rope friends!